SHINE
THE ART OF SHINING FROM WITHIN

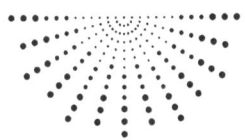

MARLYS STRADMEIJER

Copyright © 2025 by Marlys Stradmeijer and Divine Destiny Publishing.

All Rights Reserved. Apart from any fair dealing for the purposes of research or private study, or criticism or review, as permitted under the Copyright, Designs and Patents Act 1988, this publication may only be reproduced, stored or transmitted, in any form or by any means, with the prior permission in writing of the copyright owner, or in the case of the reprographic reproduction in accordance with the terms of licensees issued by the Copyright Licensing Agency. Inquiries concerning reproduction outside those terms should be sent to the publisher.

CONTENTS

Introduction	v
Foreword	vii

SOUL

1. Let the Earth Speak to You	1
2. Starfish	5
3. The Story of the Dolphins & Turtles	9
4. Soul Desire	17

HEART

5. Love Story	27
6. New Direction	33
7. My TV Dream	39
8. Self-Love	45

INTUITION

9. A Magical Experience	55
10. Intuition	59
11. Intuition at Work	63
12. Body Awareness	71
13. Intuitive Creation	75

NOW

14. The Present is a Present	85
15. Women's Retreat in Italy	91
16. The Empty Space	95
17. The Energy of Trust	99

EVOLVE

21. Speakers Academy	107
22. Growing in your comfort zone	115
23. Ancient wisdom & feminine energy	119
24. And-Also	127
25. Soul light	133

Acknowledgements	141
Gratitude	143
About the Author	145

FOREWORD

When I first met Marlys Stradmeijer, I felt like we were picking up on a conversation we had started years before.

Her warmth, wit, and curiosity are what infuse not only her personal conversations but also her writing.

Shine is a book that not only gives great insight into Marlys through her accounts of her travels and unexpected insights along the way. It also gave me insight into myself.

That's the way Marlys writes. She holds the stories of her adventures in her hands like a stone. With her written words she turns them over and over between her fingers until they're smooth, shiny, and brilliant. Then, she offers them to us to hold in our hands and hearts.

Shine is a beautiful road trip in book form. I feel like I've felt the water of the Aegean between my toes and the blades of Italian mountain grass under my head.

The questions she asks throughout the book link us all together. Each one of us who answer her questions are a link in the chain that bind us beautifully together.

It's a book you'll not only read once, but again and again. Each time you need to be reminded of who you truly are, each time you want to be transported halfway across the world, all you need to do is Shine.

Yvette Ferris

Literary Consultant

INTRODUCTION

Welcome to SHINE!

The power of shining from within.

The symbol of the sun. That was the first thing, the starting point for writing this book. There was no title and no fixed idea.

Just the beautiful image of the sun and a heart's desire to write this book. Being guided from within, by my soul light.

Writing this book was like exploring a journey, and I was the facilitator for anything this inner sun wanted to share.

And by doing that, the stories just popped up. All the stories are my authentic stories, shared from the heart.

And then, whilst writing it all fell into place. This symbol of the sun is there for a reason. All the stories shared in this book are like rays of the sun.

Connected to source. Spreading their light. To inspire and activate you to shine your light.

Shine also stands for the different categories in the book.

S: Soul

H: Heart

I: Intuition

N: Now

E: Evolve

My wish is that each of these stories will shine a light and reconnect you with your joy, playfulness and your inner wisdom. Your inner sun.

I wish you happy reading!

Lots of love,

Marlys

SOUL

> *"Traveler, there are no paths.
> Paths are made by walking."*
>
> **Antonio Machado**

1
LET THE EARTH SPEAK TO YOU

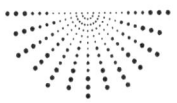

I've been visiting Mallorca since I was a child, a beautiful Spanish island in the Mediterranean, known for its turquoise waters, rugged landscapes where mountains meet the sea, and old villages with narrow streets and lively market squares. My family owned an apartment there, and now it's mine. We've spent many summers making memories on the island.

Mallorca is where I had my first *grounding* experience. When I was around seven years old, I was already a big fan of the sea. I loved to float on my back, looking at the sky and enjoying the little waves of the sea and the sun on my skin.

I remember the feeling of connection, I was so aware of my connection with the sky, the sea, Earth and everything around me.

It made me feel safe and happy.

I did not know about the word *grounding* then.

Back then I thought everyone felt that way. But when I noticed this was not the case, I kept it as my little secret, this feeling of connection.

Years later in 2013, I had a magical experience that took me to another level of *grounding*.

I was on a small Dutch island called Schiermonnikoog, on my own for a week to write my first book. The island is a nature reserve with lots of dunes and wide beaches and only one small village. No cars are allowed, so walking and cycling is the way of transport. There are no distractions, so it is a perfect spot to write. Just me, nature and my pen and paper.

That morning, I had spoiled myself with an early morning massage from a masseur on the island. Afterwards I stepped on my bike for my daily exercise. I cycled around without a special plan and allowed my intuition to be my guide.

Suddenly I noticed a small path that I did not see before, so I decided to stop and park my bike. I walked down the path, not knowing where it would lead me. Then I saw a perfect spot to lay down to relax and enjoy the sun. A small, secluded place in nature, a kind of womb made of sand, surrounded by dunes. There was no one there.

When I made myself comfortable in that perfect spot, laying down, in a completely relaxed state, I was aware of my whole body, especially after the early morning massage.

I could feel myself laying on the sand. It was soft and warm. The sun rays were gently touching my face. I felt safe and surrounded by the dunes, feeling the soft ground underneath me. I felt that I could deeply anchor my body into the Earth.

And then it happened. It was like the Earth was whispering to me. "Yes! Just surrender, surrender, surrender…"

And I did. I closed my eyes and could feel myself going deeper and deeper through the Earth.

It started with going through the surface. Then I gently fell deeper down. Going through layer by layer, deeper and deeper, until I went right through Earth! I suddenly arrived in the enormous endless space around the Earth. It did not feel scary. I felt so comfortable being there. I remember thinking, wow, of course this feels so logical!!

We are surrounded with so much more than Earth. Even though as humans we are so focused on ourselves and hardly think of planet Earth.

We surely don't realize that we are connected with so much more. But the truth is, we are. This feeling was so profound and felt like an important realization.

We are not alone. We are connected with so much more than we are aware of.

We just must be more open and willing to receive.

Since then, I have created a routine to be grateful for this connection with daily practice. Every night, just before going to sleep, I step outside and look up to the sky.

With a smile on my face, I hold my hands up high as a way of saying hello and thank you.

Sometimes the sky is filled with stars and a beautiful moon. Sometimes the sky is filled with clouds. Even when it rains, I step outside for a short moment and a quick glance at the sky. A daily reminder of the connection which is there for all of us.

Questions:

When do you feel connected with Earth and everything around you?

Think back on some situations and choose one to journal about.

Where were you?

What did you do?

How did you feel?

Where could you feel the sensation of being connected in your body?

Practice Grounding:

Feeling the Earth with bare feet

Stomping

Jumping

Dancing

Opening your senses to look, feel, smell and listen with full attention.

2
STARFISH

MY MAGICAL ENCOUNTER WITH A STARFISH.

Have you ever heard of the Octopus teacher? It's an amazing documentary on Netflix about a man's unusual friendship with an octopus in South Africa. I loved this documentary from 2020.

And I would never have thought that a couple of years later I would experience my own magical encounter with an animal in the sea.

Let me tell you my true story of how a normal day turned into a magical one.

It was in Mallorca, the biggest island of the Balearic group in Spain, where we have an apartment close to the sea.

Every day I start my day with a refreshing dive in the sea.

Preferably even before breakfast when it's still quiet and peaceful.

One morning when I walked to 'our bay', a big, secluded bay surrounded by mountains, I found myself lucky. I was the only one at the beach and I had the whole bay for myself. The sea lay before me calm and clear. Just perfect.

I had a nice swim and whilst swimming I thought about a conversation of the day before I had with a Spanish friend. We talked about the changes in nature, how the beaches used to be filled with beautiful shells and about the sea full of starfishes. We both remembered how we used to dive for starfishes in the shallow water, they were black and yellow.

We used to pick them up, admire them for a short moment and let them free again in the sea. "I have not seen a starfish in so many years" I said, "I really miss them! "

I swam to shallow water where I could stand and suddenly, I saw her. A beautiful starfish! I stood still and could not believe my eyes.

"Oh, Starfish, you are still there! I am so happy to see you!!! I heard myself-talking out loud to the starfish. My whole body was filled with gratitude, love and joy. I felt so happy. I stood still and watched her tracking in the direction of the deeper sea.

Suddenly she stood still and changed her direction towards me. I was standing with my mouth open, watching what was happening. She came closer and closer until she reached my foot.

Slowly she moved one of her arms on my red toenail. And then another one. And another arm. Until she totally sat on my foot.

I could not believe what was happening.

I could feel her tiny tube feet tickling on my foot. It felt as if she embraced me. The tears rolled over my cheeks. At that moment It felt like we were one. Connected. Time stood still. It was utterly a moment of being.

Have you ever experienced something like that?

I don't know how long we stood there in togetherness. But at a certain moment she slowly moved her five arms from my foot back into the sand and went her own way.

The whole day I felt like I was flying and filled with gratitude. I realized I would never forget this moment. It will always be a part of me. A reminder that we are all connected.

Well, this was my Octopus Teacher moment. And I am still grateful for this experience.

A year later, I found myself in the same bay. It was early in the morning. I was having my last swim in the sea, just before heading to the airport to go home. I started thinking about the story above, when I spotted a starfish. I stopped and just watched and again, something special happened. This starfish turned her path from the direction to the sea and started to move towards me. I could not believe it.

What is happening here? Was it the same starfish as last time?

The starfish came my way until she reached my feet. She went from one foot to the other, almost touching it, then slowly continued her path in between my legs. I thought, what a beautiful way of saying goodbye.

For me these wonderful things are all signs of the magic and the power of love. This goes beyond people. It also includes animals and nature in general.

I truly believe this force is so much stronger than we realize. There is more than we can see.

Don't you agree?

Questions:

Have you ever experienced something like that?

Think back on your magical moment. What pops up in your mind? What do you see, feel, hear?

Journal about your insights.

3
THE STORY OF THE DOLPHINS & TURTLES

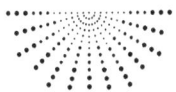

To celebrate our 25th wedding anniversary, my husband and I wanted to do something special. I instantly thought, let's go to Australia! We visited Australia before our marriage during a 6-month tour around the world and went back with our two children in celebration of our 10th wedding anniversary. So, a roundtrip through Australia would feel like the circle was round again.

Australia for us Dutchies, is really at the other end of the world. We left the Netherlands in winter, while it's summer over there. We went with our two children, who are students, and we booked a stopover in Malaysia for a two-week family road trip.

We had a great time in Malaysia as a family doing the things we all love. Traveling to places we had never been before, learning about new cultures and tasting authentic food. But most important, we were together as a family. After these two weeks it was time to say goodbye and go our own ways. My husband and I took our plane to Sydney Australia, to visit my husband's family and be there for New Years Eve.

After that it our road trip with just the two of us began. We went on a 3-day camping trip to Uluru in the outback, rented a campervan in Perth and traveled over 6000 km through West Australia. Usually after two days at one spot, we felt a desire bubbling to move and discover new places. I could write a whole book about all the things we experienced, the Aboriginals, the power of nature and the beautiful places we visited.

Let me tell you one story.

It took us until the end of our road trip, to find a place where we did not want to leave at all. Our little paradise: Monkey Mia in West Australia. It is just a little dot on the map, located at the most westerly point of the Australian continent. A bay with a beach, with a caravan park, two swimming pools, two restaurants and a little shop. But best of all are the dolphins!

Monkey Mia is part of the World Heritage Shark Bay, an International Protected National Park, of which 70 % is marine water and the habitat of many species like green turtles, one of the world's largest dugong's populations and hundreds of dolphins.

Our campervan was parked close to the sea. When we woke up in the morning our day started with a nice swim and a big possibility of seeing dolphins. Then we had a coffee at the terrace of the restaurant with a beautiful view of the turquoise sea. Our days were just perfect.

Normally Monkey Mia is packed with people, but we were

lucky, during our visit the school holidays were over, and we had the beach almost to ourselves.

Dolphins are special creatures and in many cultures a symbol for high intelligence, communication, playfulness and joy. They remind us to trust our intuition and to enjoy life fully.

Every morning a group of dolphins visit the bay, always in the same area, where a dolphin ranger gives fish to the same two dolphins, a mother and her child. The other dolphins don't get fish, they just like to be around to play. While you are standing at the beach, the dolphins swim up and down the coastline. As a visitor it is amazing to see the dolphins that close. While feeding, the ranger shares all kinds of information about the dolphins, like that they are masters in swimming in shallow water and they love to cruise along the beach. When they are hunting for fish, they can reach a speed of 40 km an hour, so you always have to watch out not to stand in their way. And they are very intelligent and can recognize faces.

When I heard that I was wondering would they recognize me?

A group of four hundred dolphins live close to the habitat of the bay. Many come to pay a visit to Monkey Mia, not only in the mornings, but also during the day. All I wanted to do all day was stay at this bay. To swim with the dolphins, to watch them. To stare over the ocean to see if they would come again, and often they did!

We could observe their behavior, hear their sounds of their breathing in and out, their communication with high peeps and little whistles. It was touching me deeply. So beautiful, playful and pure.

There was a mother with a young one, teaching her child very patiently how to catch some fish. She was pointing with her nose to the fishes, like saying: "Honey, this is all yours!"

After the phase of drinking by the mother, the little ones have to learn to do it by themselves. Because in contrast with orcas, dolphins don't share their food, they are solitary fishers.

We saw the dolphins playing, chasing each other, jumping, changing speed and hunting fish. Their favorite play was a rope of a catamaran which was attached to an anchor in shallow water.

They swam over and underneath the rope, as a nice way to massage their skin.

One day when I was snorkeling, I saw a group of dolphins in the distance. I held on to the rope of the catamaran to stay at one position, holding my face in the water. I thought maybe I would get lucky, and they would come my way? All of the sudden, four dolphins swam my way at high speed. I heard the ranger screaming at me: "Don't move!" The dolphins were passing me by my left and right side. I did not dare to move or breathe, because I didn't want to be in their way and knew I by touching them I might make them ill. It all happened so fast. When I got out of the water, I was still flabbergasted. Did this really happen?

It was something I always longed for, being so close to the dolphins, but this had happened so sudden and so fast that it was almost overwhelming. Still, it was an experience I will always remember.

Now, let me tell you about the Turtles.

Another beautiful thing about Monkey Mia are the turtles, the ancient mariners. Every night at sunset they come to visit the jetty at Monkey Mia. No idea why but they do!

When we found out about this habit, all we had to do was sit at the jetty at sunset, our legs sweeping over the edge and looking patiently at the water. And every night when we were there, various turtles came to pay a visit. We could see clearly their little heads rising above the water to breathe, their cute little round eyes, and the movements of their flippers. They came so close to where we were sitting, swimming up and down around the jetty. They were absolutely adorable.

"Mom, I have a new nickname for you", my daughter said when I told her about the turtles. "You are a turtle whisperer; they love to be where you are." It gave me a smile. My daughter and I used to play in the sea, she jumped on my back calling me a turtle. And she also referred to another experience a week before when we were snorkeling over the reef with a guided tour. Many times, I was the first one of the groups who saw turtles.

Besides that, turtles are adorable and I have a feeling they are very wise.

Did you know turtles are one of the oldest animals on Earth, over 200 million years old? They sense a kind of old wisdom that we don't know or have forgotten about. It is so relaxing to watch them, their movement is very meditative.

Being so close to the dolphins and turtles in their natural habitat was magical. Knowing it is their choice to be there, to come and play. It filled me with joy, and it was as if they had a direct line straight to my heart, touching my soul. They made me so aware of the importance of being in the now. Without expectations, enjoying each moment with all my senses, open to receive and to connect. I realized that is all I wanted to do, just to be there, in the now. To connect to myself, the environment, the sea and the stars.

We extended our initial two days stay, to four days at this beautiful place. During the rest of our road trip, we always moved after two days to explore new places. But here at Monkey Mia, we did not even want to leave to go grocery shopping.

Then it was time to say goodbye, we had to get back to Perth to return the campervan and fly back home. We felt pain in our hearts because we did not want to leave this magical place.

So, after dinner, just before going to bed when the sky was filled with stars, I said "honey, shall we go to the beach for the last time to say goodbye to the dolphins?"

When we arrived at the beach no one else was there. It was deserted and dark. The only light we could see was a strip of moonlight on the water. My husband and I talked about how grateful we both were to be there, to have experienced the dolphins and turtles so close. To have the chance to spend four days at this little paradise.

"I will miss you so much sweet dolphins" I said out loud to the water. "It would be so wonderful if you could come here to say goodbye."

And I was staring at the strip of moonlight to see if I could recognize the shape of a dolphin. Maybe they had heard or felt my wish. But nothing happened. Just the reflection of the moon in the water.

Just when we wanted to leave the beach to return to our campervan, we suddenly could hear a noise. It was definitcly a noise we could recognize well, since we had heard it so many times the past view days.

It was the noise of dolphins breathing. I immediately had goose bumps all over. "Oh dolphin." I said with a tear in my eye. "You heard me. You did come to say goodbye!" We could hear how the dolphin was swimming really close to where we were standing at the beach. We could see its movements in the water showing that the dolphin was swimming a couple of times up and down where we were standing. And then it swam away in the darkness of the ocean. It had touched my soul on a deep level. I felt so connected. This is a feeling I will always hold in my heart.

Questions:

Have you ever been to a place that you did not want to leave?

What was it about that trip that lit up your soul?

With what kind of animals do you feel connected?

4
SOUL DESIRE

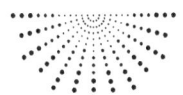

Do you have a big desire, but you don't dare to listen to it? I have met many people with a dream, a big desire that is often kept away. It can pop up now and then. But most people quickly get back on track. Living the life that they know, a life that feels comfortable. Not ready to make the big jump out of the comfort zone. We tell ourselves all kinds of things to stay exactly where we are in the comfort zone, because we are afraid of the unknown. Maybe we feel we are not ready for it yet, or our desire is not realistic. So, we prefer to defer our dreams.

What we don't realize is the effect of it, we keep our dreams far away, hidden in our personal secret treasure box. We just go on living life, wondering why time is slipping through our fingers. Do you know this feeling?

I know this from experience. And how frustrating it can be, especially when you have a clear vision about your dream.

The luck to know what your heart desires, but not the courage to listen and take action.

Let me tell you my story.

I changed direction in 2006 from working as a communication manager at a big company, to becoming a coach in personal development. I was lucky to find my mission in life. As part of my education to become a coach, we as students were clients first, in order to learn the effect of the practices firsthand. One very powerful guided visualization that we learned was about finding your soul mission. In this guided visualization I first had to connect with my heart and to climb a high mountain. To reach the top I had to overcome all kinds of obstacles under way, just like in many films and video games. Anyway, I survived this mission and finally found myself on top of the mountain. While I was enjoying the beautiful view, something special happened: I received a gift from my higher self. A gift that would represent my soul mission.

What did I get?

It was a treasure box. A beautiful one. The top was covered with gems in all kinds of colors. I was so happy with this present. But the true gift was inside. When I opened this treasure box, an immense light spread out.

Bright like the sun.

It was speechless. I thought, WOW, this is huge.

My soul mission is to SHINE!

I could feel goosebumps all over my body and a big yes from my heart. I knew this was the truth. And then a vision popped up, an invitation to write a book about it. The title will be the Art of Shining from Within. It's going to be a journey filled with discoveries that I am going to share.

This idea filled me with so much joy. But then when I arrived back home, I did all kinds of things, I started my coaching company and took care of my children, but no writing.

Yes, I was collecting a lot of information that could be interesting for the book, but I was not able to write anything out on paper.

Many years passed by. I did not forget about the desire to write this book, but to be honest with you, fear was stopping me. The fear of not being good enough to write, that the subject would not be understood. Fear that I was not ready and not knowing where to begin.

Did you ever let fear stop you from doing the thing you desired?

So, my life went on. Until one day the universe decided to give me a kick in the ass to show me what I was doing.

It was a summer day in 2012. My husband and I, along with our two children, were spending our holiday in Thailand.

In Bangkok, we booked a guided tour on bicycles to see more of the city with a private guide, just for the four of us. I love this way of exploring a new environment on a bike, seeing the city through the eyes of a local.

Our guide took us to all kinds of places. We cycled through markets, small roads, little canals and hidden gems of the city where you normally don't come as a tourist. We saw many temples. One of them was very special. "Here you see the oldest temple from Bangkok," our guide said. "It's a temple with wishing bells on the ceiling. The bells are placed there by people with a big wish. So, if you have a big wish, this is your chance!" We took off our shoes and went silently inside. I could feel the serene atmosphere inside and there were many white wishing bells on the ceiling.

While my family passed on their way to see more of the temple. I stood there frozen. I could really feel my heart's desire. It was filling my entire body. Then suddenly sadness came over me because I realized, what if I continue to not take action toward my heart's desire. What if I die without even trying to write a book?

I knew this was definitely not what I wanted as my future, feelings of disappointment and sadness. I was living my life as one of the lucky ones, knowing what my heart desired and not having the courage to listen to it.

So, I put some money in the box, chose a nice-looking wishing bell, connected with my heart and soul desire and hung my wishing bell from the ceiling.

And at that moment something happened. A moment of clarity.

I needed to change my question! It is not: What do I need to write this book?

The true question is: What does this book need to see the light?

For me the answer was: I need to write this book together with someone else. So, we can make the journey more fun, and this co-author can give me a kick under the butt when needed.

Two weeks later, when we were back home, I was asked to join a lecture about philosophy. The presenter was a woman, and whilst listening to her, my intuition was telling me: "This woman is interesting for you."

I had no idea, but I decided to listen to my intuition and take action. I took the chance to go talk to her, even though she might laugh at me or think that I am a fool. I told her about my gut feeling.

We had coffee the next day, although it was a nice conversation, I still had no idea what my intuition wanted to tell me. After one hour, we almost said goodbye. I told her about my heart's desire to write a book called, *The Art of Shining From Within.*

She started to shine herself and said, "you know what? "I am not only a philosopher, but I also have a publishing company!

May I write this book with you, and publish it?"

Wow!!!

That's where the journey of my first book started to take form. In 2013, one year later the book was published in Dutch.

De Kunst van het Stralen. A book with interviews, exercises and some personal stories of my co-author and me. It was wonderful to make this dream come true, and the media loved it.

We gave workshops about the book, presentations and interviews. I was so happy I had the courage to listen to my soul desire and take action.

Because that is what I love to do. To inspire you to find your soul mission and to manifest it. So, you can shine your light!

And now, over a decade has passed and as you are reading this, I listened to a new big soul desire. The next step: my first solo book, in English. I wanted to share my own authentic truth and knowledge about the art of shining from within. To shine my soul light and inspire you to do the same.

Question:

Do you have a soul desire?

Exercise:

Visualize that you are in this temple in Bangkok. Feel your feet on the ground. Breathe in and out.

Connect with your heart and feel your soul desire.

Now it's time to hang your wishing bell on the ceiling…

How does it feel?

Be with this for a while and then take your journal and write about it.

What does your soul desire need in order to come true?

HEART

*"Wherever your heart is,
there you find your treasures."*
Paolo Coelho

5
LOVE STORY

Love is one of the most interesting topics ever. It's the inspiration for novels, movies, art and so much more.

In our Saturday newspaper my favorite read is always a column about love. It contains weekly insights and an interview with a person about their experience with love, the power of love, and the wonderful coincidences of meeting the ones we love.

Isn't it always wonderful to hear how two people meet, somewhere in the world, right at that moment, and Cupid's arrow follows right in their heart?

Sometimes, I wonder if there's an orchestration, like meeting someone right at that moment in your life. Usually, the question that follows always has to do with trust. Does it often feel a bit scary to open your heart to someone? Because when you do, you also have the chance that it might break. Trust is definitely an essential base for love.

Let me tell you my love story.

When I was in my twenties, I was a career woman working at a big company in Amsterdam in communications. It was holiday time, and together with a dear friend I went to the island Kos, a popular island in Greece for nine days. We rented some bikes and cycled three hours, all the way to the other side of the island to get out of the busy crowd and to find a beautiful quiet beach. We found one, a hidden treasure as you sometimes see in magazines. A small secluded sandy beach with some parasols and sunbeds. It had beautiful clear blue water.

We went for a refreshing swim when I suddenly saw a very nice-looking guy standing on the pier looking out over the sea. He was tall, dark haired with a sportive posture. He looked Italian or maybe Greek.

Anyway, he had spotted me as well. When I got out of the water, to my surprise, he spoke to me in Dutch! "Do you know it's raining in the Netherlands right now?"

"Oh no," I replied. We cycled all the way to the other side of the island to get away from all the Dutch tourists, and here you are!"

We started laughing and talking. Nonstop. We completely lost track of time. Our hands were totally wrinkled from the seawater.

Was this a well-orchestrated meeting by our souls? Something that needed to happen? Right there, at that moment?

He was only there for six days. He and my friend also got along really well. We had fun with the three of us, but nothing happened until the last two days. Then we finally kissed and had a short summer romance. At the end of the holiday, we said goodbye thinking we would probably not see each other again.

But more had happened to us than we had realized. Back home people asked both of us. "What has happened to you? Are you in love or something? You are glowing from ear to ear!!"

We stepped into a long-distance romance. The next weekend I was back home, he drove all the way from Switzerland to the Netherlands, a twelve-hour drive, just to be with me for a weekend. We had a wonderful time and realized that we were deeply in love.

For one year we had a long-distance romance, meeting each other once a month, in various places. We met in Paris, France, Milano, Italy and Heidelberg, Germany which was exactly halfway between Switzerland and the Netherlands. It was perfect for a year, but after that year things did not flow anymore. Something needed to change. It was like we had arrived at a crossing point, where we had to make a choice. Shall we stop our relationship? Or continue? But how and where?

We knew we could not go on this way. We were both ready for the next step. Shall we stay or shall we go? That was the question.

Have you ever been in a crossing point where you know you had to choose something but had no idea what? Like in an impossible split?

We planned a weekend away to get some more clarity in our choices and possibilities, hoping we could find a solution that we had not thought of before. The best place to brainstorm was in nature. We went to a beach, looking over the wide sea. We started talking about our wishes, our fears, the things we most dreamt off. From there we started brainstorming about possibilities.

We came to the conclusion that the next phase in our relationship needed a fresh start for both of us. Starting from the same base. Our creative adventurous plan was to quit our jobs and buy a ticket around the world! We would be backpacking and traveling together for six months. A great way to get to know each other better, to deepen our relationship and to see if it worked. We both had saved money, had no kids, no obligations. We quickly realized, if this is our big desire, this is the moment to go for it.

Would we really dare to jump in the deep?

At that time the economics in Europe were not great and there was a lot of unemployment in the Netherlands. We both had a career and a well-paid job, so it definitely took some courage to leave all of that behind. It felt like a big jump in the unknown. I realized that the worst-case scenario was that our whole adventure would be a fiasco. Where I would come home, heartbroken, without a relationship and without a job. Would I really want to take that risk?

My heart decided Yes, you do. This is exactly the risk I had to take. To say yes to love and to find out if he's the one. And even if you look at the worst-case scenario, just trust that you can handle it. You will find a new job. Although it will hurt a lot, you will survive a broken heart, even though it will be tough.

So, we both jumped into our new adventure together.

Our ticket around the world brought us from Singapore to several islands in Indonesia, where I learned to dive. We did several dives together which was amazing to explore the underwater world with each other as a dive buddy.

We visited Joost's family in Sydney Australia, bought an old Ford Falcon and traveled all the way up from Sydney to Cairns. Enjoyed the beauty of the Great Barrier Reef. Sold the car at the end of our road trip in Australia for a good price and used the money to fly back to Sydney.

Then we went to New Zealand where we bought an old hippy campervan with colored curtains and traveled around the North and South island.

We saw orca's, walked in ancient woods and enjoyed the most beautiful sceneries.

We saw a lot and shared many experiences together. It's true, being together 24/7, we definitely got to know each other better!

When we came back home for our trip, there was no doubt at all. We knew we wanted to live together.

A couple of months later to my surprise I caught the wedding bouquet of a dear friend. Shortly after that Joost asked me to marry him.

We have been married for over twenty-five years, with two children and a lovely life.

To tell you the truth, these six months traveling together, taking the risk of losing everything, listening to our hearts and intuition, has proved to be the best foundation for our relationship. It was the best choice we could have ever made.

Questions:

What is your relationship with love?

Have you ever taken a step into the unknown, trusting your heart and intuition?

Exercise:

Just think of a person or an animal you truly love. Take 3 deep breaths in and out and let that energy of love flow through your body, like a river

How does that feel?

6
NEW DIRECTION

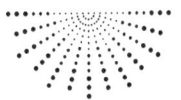

ARE YOU READY FOR A NEW DIRECTION IN LIFE?

Sometimes in life you are on a certain track that seems comfortable. But then something happens that turns your world upside down. A pivotal moment.

A moment that asks you to take a second look at your life. Are you still heading in the right direction?

I experienced this moment in 2002. We had just moved from Amsterdam to a different town closer to the dunes and the sea. It was a nice old house with lots of renovation work to do.

Our newborn boy, our second child, was just a couple of months old. I was still breast feeding him when I returned to work as a communication manager at a company in Amsterdam.

Because of that I always had to run to catch the train on time, and to use the breaks at work to tap my milk for my little one with a small machine. It was a busy life with broken and sleepless nights. I felt like I was running all the time. Trying to juggle way too many balls in the air.

What I know now, but did not realize then, I was asking too much of myself and of my body. I was trying to be the perfect mom, the perfect wife, and the perfect employee, to be there for everyone, like a big people pleaser.

But I hardly found time to rest and to reflect. As a busy mom with small children, I had no ME time at all.

And one day, it happened. My energy dropped to zero. Whilst cooking I literally could not stand on my feet anymore and fell on the floor.

My body said: "ENOUGH"!

Did you ever have a pivotal moment that you knew something had to change?

Of course I went to see a doctor. And she said I really had to rest, "You are having a burnout and if you don't slow down, you will get worse."

Lucky for me, some people came to help. At home, laying on the couch, I was thinking; "how could this have happened to me? Me, Marlys who usually is so full of energy. What went wrong? Which signals did I ignore?"

I decided then and there to make a promise to my body. From now on, I will listen. I will listen to what it wants to tell me, even when it's a whisper. I realized that I needed to learn more about my body language.

When I felt better, I followed all kinds of training about body awareness. I learned about body language and Shiatsu, an Asian body work form of massage.

I learned a lot about checking in on a regular basis with myself.

After a couple of months, a coincidence happened. It was an invitation to change direction. I am always aware of coincidences. Because aren't they like a little miracle? I see them as guiding lights on our journey.

I met a woman at a congress about personal development, organized by friends. She gave us a presentation about following your dream by using your inner power.

I listened to her with awe, while my heart was jumping from joy. I can say this was definitely a body signal that I wasn't going to ignore.

So, after her presentation, I walked to the speaker's desk and waited for a moment to talk to her.

I said to her, "Thank you for your presentation. I loved it and I was wondering, how did you come to do what you do? Where did you learn this?"

She enthusiastically told me about the two years of education she had done for counseling and coaching where creativity, body, mind and soul were integrated.

Back home I read more about it and felt a big Yes. And it all fell into place. I was just on time. Classes started two weeks later, and they were on the weekend, it was perfect.

When my husband saw my joy and enthusiasm. He said, "Honey, do it. We can and will make this work."

A New Direction

I attended classes for 1 ½ years. I loved everything I learned there. All different kinds of coaching techniques for job coaching and personal development. I learned how the body, mind and soul can work together, and the power of visualization. Including various techniques to help people reconnect with their inner treasure box.

One exercise was to visualize your dream job. This is a way to get more clarity on a conscious and unconscious level about your deepest desires. When another coach was giving me this exercise, I could see and feel clearly what I wanted. Then I had to make a drawing from what I had seen. I could see myself being so happy working close to home in a little house, surrounded by nature. Doing the work I love. Inspiring people to reconnect with their inner wisdom and guiding them in their most fulfilling life. For me, it was a fulfilling work job without stress. It was my own coaching practice which I could easily combine with being a mother.

And guess what, everything I had drawn on paper came true!

A few months later I started my coaching practice in a charming house near a park close to home with an affordable rent. So, no stress of traffic jams or trains running late. I could easily walk to my work and on top of that I could organize my own schedule.

A new life had begun. I loved my work, my energy was back,

and my family and I flourished. You can certainly say, I was back on track.

This change in career could not have been better. Every year I took a course to grow professionally which I loved, because my personal development has always been important to me. Being a coach, I could share everything I learned with my clients, and I also learned from them. I grew professionally and personally and so did they. We learned how to listen to our mind, body and spirit. We learned how to connect with our inner wisdom and allow dreams in our lives and make them come true. We also learned how to be our most authentic self and live life fully.

You can definitely say that the burnout, when my body could not carry me anymore, was an awful moment in my life, but it certainly made me aware of something very important.

A lesson that I will never forget. My picture of being miss perfect had to change. Instead of non-stop giving to others, I also had to give to myself and take care of me.

By taking good care of myself, my body and my energy level, I am a much nicer person and able to give so much more. And most importantly, by living my life in connection with body, mind and soul, I live life fully, authentically and shine my light. So that I can be an inspiration for others to do the same, a guiding light.

Questions:

When you look back at your life, what kind of pivotal moments did you have?

How did they affect your life?

How did you make your choices?

Coincidences:

Become more aware of coincidences happening in your life. They might be stepping stones or guiding lights for your journey.

Journal about some coincidences that you remember.

7
MY TV DREAM

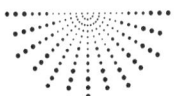

My coaching practice was flourishing, and I loved my work. I was guiding my clients to be more connected with themselves so they could make choices from their heart.

To combine their body, mind and soul in work and life in general.

My clients often initially came to me with a work-related question, like: "What do I really want? How can I stand in my power? What is stopping me?"

Also questions like, "why do I feel so low in energy, and full of doubts? What do I need to shine again?"

Finding their way to be more connected to their body, mind and soul was having a positive effect on many aspects of their personal life, work, and relationships. Because when the sun starts to shine inside, its rays are touching everyone around.

And when my clients opened up to their heart desires, to see, feel and receive, many dreams were fulfilled. Like the dream of a client that was not happy in his job as manager at a big company. He had tried to rationalize his next steps but could not find a solution on how to live a heart-aligned life. In an exercise I started with a short meditation and then guided him through a visualization to get in touch with his heart desires. He saw his big forgotten dream, of having his own restaurant. After the visualization, I asked him to make a drawing of it. By doing so, we were giving his dream room to be so the magic could happen. He started to shine all over and could feel it in his body. He started to talk about it with an open mind, seeing all kinds of possibilities.

In the next coaching sessions, we worked on the question of what was stopping him and to clear the road for his dream.

One year later I received a postcard in the mail with a picture in front of a nice restaurant at a waterfront. It was exactly as he had visualized! "Thank you so much, do you remember my drawing? My dream came true!!"

Incredible things can happen after giving full room to your heart desires. As if the whole universe conspires to make it real.

Let me tell you the story of my forgotten dream.

On the last day of my education to become a coach, my teacher gave a guided visualization to get more clarity on my desires in working as a life coach.

To my surprise, I remember seeing a combination of two words, coaching and television.

I had no idea what it actually meant, or how to combine these two. But the idea of coaching on TV was exciting and made me very happy.

I could feel it in my body, and I remember it also made me laugh. I started thinking, what was happening here? I had forgotten about my childhood dream to work for TV, and here it popped up again.

Three months later, the phone rang. "Hello, I am Philip from national TV. Is it correct that you are a coach?" I remember it was April 1, Fools Day and I actually thought somebody was pranking me.

So, I said, "thank you for calling, but I really must go now. If you want, you can call me again in one hour. Have a nice day."

One hour later, I remember I was at the swimming pool where my children were having swimming classes, the phone rang again.

It was Philip, he found me on the internet. He asked me if I was interested in becoming the mental coach for a new series on National TV.

I was totally in shock, but in a good way. Wow, the power of that visualization is working! To me this whole story so far was a winning game, but there was more to come.

He said, "the next step is a job interview with the director of TV and you have to compete with two hundred other coaches. During the job interview the cameras will roll to see how you perform on TV."

To calm myself before the job interview, I was coaching myself. Saying: "just see this whole day as an adventure, you have nothing to lose. This is a wonderful experience. Picture yourself as a rabbit, who may sniffle at a TV studio!"

And it worked, I was relaxed during the job interview and enjoyed every moment. I did get the job. The Director and Producer chose me!

A couple of months, a new adventure started, I was the mental coach on TV for a new series of programs.

Be aware of what you wish for!

Yes, I did get the job. But coaching on TV was quite challenging. I had to deal with my clients, a group of men, and a whole TV crew. Before recording, a woman did my hair and makeup. There were two camera men, a producer, a director and a floor manager. My clients were nervous to be live on TV. It was a rather unusual setting to coach.

I felt like I had to take care of my clients and myself. In order to perform in the best way possible, it was important to invite myself to be authentically me, and to help my clients to do the same. To feel comfortable and relaxed. To trust the coaching process and not to be distracted by the cameras.

Every day before we started, I went to the restroom to have a few minutes for myself to do a grounding exercise. I imagined I was a tree, with deep roots in the ground and I took a couple of deep breaths in and out. It worked.

The clients were happy, and the series of programs was a success.

The biggest feeling of success for me however was proof that miracles do happen when you allow yourself to dream. The power of visualization can be massive.

Questions:

Do you have a dream? Something you would love to do or realize?

What do you do to create space for your dream?

Suggestions to keep your dream alive, you can:

- Visualize your dream
- Draw a picture of your dream
- Journal about your dream
- Make a vision board of your dream

8
SELF-LOVE

"Honey, you got to adorn yourself!"

I heard a woman say this and it made me smile. She said it with so much enthusiasm, and it immediately resonated with me. Yes, this is so true.

It was on a Monday, and she was wearing a black blazer with sparkles perfectly matching her outfit, a purse, and some glamorous earrings. "You look lovely," I said! Do you have a special occasion? Something to celebrate?"

She started to smile and said: "No, I don't. Actually, it is an ordinary day, but I just love to dress this way. I am sometimes called a raven, because I just love glitter and beautiful clothes."

You are so right I said. "You just have to adorn yourself!!"

Seeing her made me happy. And I realized what she does on a

daily basis is give a present to herself. By truly seeing herself and allowing herself to wear the things that make her happy.

Not caring about or being blocked by social rules or how you should dress on an ordinary day. As if you are only aloud to shine on a special occasion.

To tell you the truth, I also love to adorn myself daily, in my own way. Every morning before jumping in the shower I think and feel into what I want to wear that day. I check in on my needs and wishes. What style will support me that day, do I feel like something colorful, dark or bright? Something comfy, chic, elegant or sportive? And what kind of material do I want to feel?

Of course, the plans of the day also are leading in a way. But the most important thing to me is how the clothes are going to make me feel that day.

How can they support me in the best way? Then I look in the mirror and as a final touch I put on my earrings, rings and sometimes a special necklace.

To tell you my guilty pleasure: I love jewelry, especially jewelry that I buy in little stores during my travels. To me they are the perfect souvenirs, easy to pack in my luggage. And most important, every time I put them on, it lights up my day and reminds me of the places I have visited and the happy feeling I had when I found them in a little store or market. I call them my little treasures.

They really don't have to cost much, but I cherish them. And on top of that, they give me my own authentic signature.

To me it is my perfect way to start the day. As a daily celebration of the day and an action of self-love.

Adorning yourself is all about celebrating yourself. The fact is that so many people have lost that ability. They even find it hard to love themselves as they are.

I once heard of an exercise in which you stand in front of a mirror, telling your reflection the words: "I love You." So many people find this extremely hard to say to themselves. Isn't that a sad thing? And why is it so hard to do?

Can you say "I love you" to your reflection in the mirror?

Inner Critic

During our lives we all have developed an inner critic, an inner voice who is always there with a spicy opinion. Your inner critic tells you how you should look and behave. And what you could have done better.

Some people even have such a strong critic inside that they are in fact nonstop punishing themselves with their self-thoughts. As a result, they find it hard to say or think something positive about themselves.

We were not born with this inner critic. A baby is innocent and pure. Just imagine if you would say all these negative things to a newborn baby. Wouldn't that be awful?

So why would we do this to ourselves?

Why do we have this inner critic?

We all developed one during the process of growing up. The main reason is to help us and protect us. But the reality is that we often give this inner critic too much power. As if it is ruling our world.

This is why it is important to be aware of your perspective toward yourself. How you are looking at yourself and the things you are saying to yourself. It can be very interesting, maybe even shocking, if you could record all these inner thoughts. And to realize how many of these thoughts are not empowering at all.

What if you could look at yourself from a more positive perspective? Like you would do with a dear friend or a child. What do you see? And what would you say?

What if you stop comparing yourself with other people and loosen up the strict strings of your self-criticism?

Be honest with yourself, is your inner critic supporting you in the way you want?

I have learned a great coaching technique called *Voice Dialogue*, to work with these inner advisors, such as the inner critic.

A clarifying way to look at the variety of inner advisors is to imagine yourself in a *bus*.

You are the driver and inside are all kinds of passengers: men, women, young and old. All with their own characteristics. These passengers are your private advisors.

Every inner advisor has a specific role. Like a Pusher, a Perfectionist, a Rebel and a Dreamer

With Voice Dialogue you get a chance to get more insights into what these inner advisors have to share with you. Who is on your bus? Which advisors are most prominent?

It can be very interesting also to pay attention to the voices that don't sit at the front of the bus, they might have an important message for you. After listening to your various advisors, you can truly make your own informed decisions to live your life in the best way possible.

So, it is important to realize what you are telling yourself daily. To be aware of the tone, the words, and the impact. To practice some self-love and self-care daily. This will certainly have a positive effect on you and the way you feel about yourself. And on top of that, you will be a positive example for the world around you.

Questions:

What do you do to adorn yourself?

Are you allowing yourself to shine without a special occasion?

Can you say *I LOVE YOU* to your self-reflection?

What could you do to practice more self-love daily?

INTUITION

*"Magic is believing in yourself,
if you can do that,
you can make anything happen."*
Johann Wolfgang Goethe

9
A MAGICAL EXPERIENCE IN ITALY

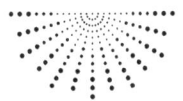

One day I was on holiday with my family in Italy. We were exploring the island Sicily, a beautiful island in the Mediterranean Sea. Besides the astonishing nature, hidden bays and little old villages with tiny streets, the island is filled with old ancient history. Such as the 'Valle dei Templi' with seven Ancient Greek Temples from around 5th century B.C.

We had already traveled around the island for ten days, enjoying the Italian coffee, food and ice creams and visiting these amazing temples. One morning while making plans for the day, I was checking a tour guidebook. Then my eye fell on a tiny text, and I could feel a sensation within my body. My intuition told me: That is the place you must go: Erice.

Erice was not a hot spot at all. A little village with a castle and some leftovers from a temple for Aphrodite/Venus. But I loved the description: "Erice is like an eagles' nest on top of a mountain."

"Hey guys, I have a nice idea for today. It is not a famous temple, but I just have the feeling we need to go there. Is that all right?" So, there we went. I was excited without knowing what would come. We drove the small road all the way up to the mountain. I trusted my intuition and was curious what it would bring me.

Did you ever go somewhere intuitively?

When we arrived at the top of the mountain, the view was spectacular over the Tyrannic Sea en the Egadi islands. My special interest however was to learn more about the leftovers of the temple. What kind of temple was it. Why was it built there? And what did it have to tell me?

I read that this temple on the top of this mountain, used to be the magical place where high priestesses gathered to hold ceremonies in honor of Aphrodite the god of virtuality, sexuality, beauty and life. Unfortunately, as often happens, the sacred place was destroyed in name of the church. Forbidding to practice these rituals ever again, claiming they were sinful and dangerous.

By doing this, the church suppressed sovereign female energy, passion and power. The beautiful female energies that were initially honored and celebrated right here at the temple. Because in name of the church they were telling women that sexuality and freedom was sinful. And they told all limiting rules about how women should dress and behave.

As a climax of masculine power and suppression, The Normans built a big Castle, right on that sacred spot. This is a thing that happened in many places. Churches and castles are often built on magical spots used by other religions.

Upon wandering around, I found my heart jumped with joy when I saw the leftovers of the old female temple. I stopped for a moment to imagine how it would have been to live there at that time. What a beautiful temple it must have been. A powerful place for women to gather.

I wondered, would I still be able to feel some of the energy that used to be there?

While my family was going to see the castle, I had different plans. "Where do you want me to go?" I asked my intuition. I walked a bit around and felt drawn to a big block of marble. I sat on it and felt an urge to lay down. I closed my eyes. And then it happened. It felt like I was making a journey into time and space. Spacious. It was not frightening at all. I was totally relaxed.

It was magical. I arrived in a place without boundaries. I could feel so much love and felt so welcome. I experienced a huge feeling of connection with everything and everyone around me. It felt like coming home to a place where I came from. Where we all came from. Source.

The tears were rolling down my cheeks. I completely lost my sense of time and space. I felt a sense of oneness. Of completeness. Of belonging.

It felt so good. I wanted to stay there forever but knew it was not my time yet. I needed to go back to real life.

To tell you the truth, I have no idea how long I was in that space. But when I opened my eyes, everything was normal around me. I could see my family and some Japanese tourists packed with cameras taking photos from the castle. I heard children laughing and playing. I was happy to see that no one was looking awkward at me. I slowly came back to normal life. With a big smile on my face. I had felt so much love, it had lightened up my soul. I took some deep breaths in and out, felt my feet on the ground and said thank you for this wonderful experience.

What happened to me there? I can't explain it rationally, it was beyond that. It definitely was an experience that amplified me and reminded me that we are not alone. We are all connected with source, and we don't have to be afraid of death. What I had experienced there was an inner wisdom, an inner knowing: this is where we all come from. This is where we go back to when life on Earth is over. There is an infinite love and connection for all of us.

Questions:

How did it make you feel reading this story?

Did you ever go somewhere because your intuition told you so?

Which memories come up?

10
INTUITION

Intuition is an interesting thing. We all have it, but I often hear people say they have lost their connection with it.

How about you? Do you listen to your intuition?

To me, my intuition is extremely important. It is my inner compass that helps me in decision making and with my direction in life. By using it regularly, the inner connection gets stronger, and you can receive insights and information. So, let us explore intuition a bit more.

What is intuition and why is it important to be more aware of your intuition?

"Intuition, according to the Cambridge Dictionary, is an ability to understand or know something without needing to think about it or use reason to discover it, or a feeling that shows this ability."

What comes up for you when you think about your intuition? Are you aware of your intuitive signals and do you dare to trust them? For example, do you have the experience that when you think about a person and then suddenly the phone rings and exactly that person is calling you? Or your intuition gives you a warning signal not to cross a road, and right after that a dangerous situation occurs with a car driving too fast.

Thinking about my intuition, I remember a special moment some years ago. Our 19-year-old daughter was backpacking in Thailand with a friend, for the first time. She was just a couple of days away. When one night, just before going to sleep, I suddenly felt the need to check my phone. Usually, I do not use my phone for 1 hour before going to bed. Our daughter had just sent a message. "I am in a hospital, I am ok, but I just had a scooter accident."

I ran to my husband to tell him the news. And we immediately sent her a message. "Are you able to speak? Shall we facetime?" "Oh, yes please!!" she answered.

She was in hospital, still in shock because of the accident. A doctor and nurse were checking her injuries. Her legs were open and needed stitches. So, we enjoyed facetime. The wonderful thing was that despite the distance, we could be there for her when she needed us most.

After a week she could continue her adventure. I was so happy my intuition had given me that signal and that I listened to it. And to be honest, it was also a big challenge for us as parents in letting her go. When we first heard about the accident, we wanted to take the first plane to Thailand to be with her. But she was a grown-up woman, and we had faith in her.

Intuition is a beautiful unconscious system that can help us in many ways. Like warning us when there is something wrong, but also when there are great opportunities ahead. Did you know your intuition can also help you in your career?

Let me tell you another story.

One day I was on my bike, cycling though the city center. We dutchies love riding bicycles. In fact, it is our most popular way of transport, especially for short distances.

It was a beautiful day; the sun was shining, and I was on my way back home. When suddenly my intuition started to speak to me. I felt a kind of bubbly feeling that came over me. Unexpectedly.

I remember being conscious of the signals and asking myself, shall I stop cycling or not? To tell you the truth, I was curious and decided to stop my bike to see what had caused it. I looked around me. Where did it come from?

I suddenly saw that I had just passed a Radio Station which I had not seen before. I started to giggle, yes, that must have been it!

I suddenly saw the picture and the pieces fell together. Right in front of me was an interesting opportunity! You see, I had just published my first book, and I had one copy of the book with me. Would this radio station be interested in my story? And would I have the courage to ask them?

To make a long story short. I listened to my intuition and decided to take action. My curiosity won over my fear. So, I parked my bike, stepped into the entrance of the radio station, and popped up my question.

And my intuition was right!

They invited me with open arms at the radio station and loved to hear more about the topic. The next morning, I was live on the radio with an interview about my book.

So, yes, I can certainly encourage you to listen to your intuition. To be open and receptive to what it might tell you. To learn to trust it, to play with it. As your inner compass in life. And to have the courage to take action.

It is just like learning something new. You just have to practice. The more open you are to receive intuitive guidance, the more your intuition will guide you on your way.

Think back to a situation when your intuition was telling you something.

Questions:

What did it tell you?

Did you listen?

Are you aware of your body signals when your intuition is on?

Where do you feel it?

11
INTUITION AT WORK

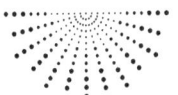

Sometimes meeting somebody enlightens something that needs to be shared. A topic that I need to write about. This happened to me recently.

On a Saturday I was invited to a friend's birthday dinner party. The guests were of various ages and when I mingled between the guests I had some nice conversations. I was especially interested in talking with some young people who just moved from being students to being professionals. When you just start somewhere new, your sight is still clear and fresh. So, I was curious about their observations. How did they experience working life?

Although the younger ones were working in different professions, they were all working in strategic fields. In every conversation strategic thinking was their key phrase. I was wondering if this was just a coincidence or is strategic thinking seen as the key to success?

Success and strategic thinking often imply that it is good to have a clear vision of where you want to go. As going in a straight line from A to B.

Thinking rationally, analytically and clearly.

What if you think differently? What if you are a person with strong intuition?

Is there room for that in corporate life? Or in the field where you work when strategic thinking is the key?

At the dinner party a young lady shared a story with me, which reminded me of how I felt during my first years in corporate life. Feeling like the odd man out, the strange duck in the pond, being highly sensitive and intuitive. Her experience had made her feel vulnerable, a feeling that we often keep out of the office. I felt honored that she felt safe enough to share it with me.

For six months she had been working at a big company in a competitive field where clear goal setting and analytical thinking were the norm.

She was invited to be part of a corporate Management Team meeting of mainly men to listen to some presentations. She told me she could usually handle her colleagues well and she had learned how to interact and to adjust. However, while she was listening to the presentation, at a certain point she intuitively knew something said was not right. That something had to change and that there was a better solution.

The problem was, she knew it intuitively, but could not find the words YET to explain it.

Even though she tried to share her intuitive idea, it did not work.

And suddenly she felt completely misunderstood. Having all these critical eyes of the boarding room looking at her. And the thing she was most afraid of happened. She started to cry. Her worst-case scenario.

On top of that, her inner critical voice started immediately to interfere. Asking herself questions like: what do they think of me? And how embarrassing. She felt like she wanted to run away or find a place in the ground to disappear.

Some colleagues gave her tissues asking, "Are you o.k."? Trying to calm her, and not really knowing what to do. Quickly as possible, they went on with business as usual.

I heard her story with admiration. Thinking wow, this woman was very brave. She had this intuitive feeling, an idea that still was in its infancy and she had the courage to speak about it. Most people don't, out of a fear of feeling foolish, being made fun or being misunderstood.

What usually happens after such an experience, we keep our mouth shut. Especially in an environment where there is no room for emotions and intuition. Correction, in an environment where we think, assume that there is no room for emotions and intuition. But this might not be truth. Intuition is usually just not mentioned.

So, after such an experience as this young woman had, there is a big chance her intuitive ideas will not be born. Because we all adjust, we go on with business as usual, thinking this is the way to proceed. Then we transfer these unwritten rules and behaviors to new employees. Leaving no room for intuitive thinking in the workplace.

What if we would give more room for intuition at work? Even if we don't know YET what it will bring exactly. Even when we cannot explain it precisely. Even if it is just a little seed without knowing what it will become.

When we realize that 80% of our communication is NON-VERBAL and we primarily focus on the minority of 20% verbal. That means that 80 % of our communication is sourced and expressed without words. For example, by facial expressions, gestures, body language and loudness or tone of voice. But by focusing on only the verbal rational part of our communication, we let go of this huge treasure box of information. Including intuitive ideas, creativity and knowledge.

What if we could use that? And be more open to the non-rational knowledge. Just imagine what amount of creativity will be available all of a sudden!

I see intuitive ideas as seeds from which it might be unclear of what is inside or what it might become. You never know, each seed might have a great treasure inside.

So, it is definitely worthwhile to see what these seeds need in order to grow. To prepare the best environment so the seeds full of possibilities and hidden treasures get the chance to be expressed and flourish. I believe the seeds filled with your intuitive ideas need a good **POT**.

Below is my **POT** theory.

POT stands for:

Playing

Open

Trust

P: The energy of Playing is good for many things. It allows people to be relaxed, to get in a flow. To try things out. To play, think out of the box.

O: An Open attitude is very helpful in the intuitive and creative process. As if anything is welcome.

T: Trust in the process. That it's absolutely o.k. not to know the outcome YET. Not to know the ins and outs of the idea YET. To give it some time to grow.

A good question is always. What does your 'seed' need to grow?

What can you do to facilitate it?

Like the case with the story of the young lady. I told her please don't see what happened to you as a failure. As if you did something wrong. This situation presents an opportunity for growth. To take care of what you need. This does not mean hiding away your intuition. No, I would advise you to investigate for yourself what would have been helpful for you in this situation. What did you need?

For example, mentioning you have an intuitive idea, and you need some more time to figure it out. To get more clarity on it.

To write it down and get back to it when you have more clarity.

Or maybe you would prefer to brainstorm with somebody about it?

Would it be helpful to go for a walk?

She could have said, "I have an intuitive feeling that there might be another solution. I don't have it clear yet but let me think about it. I will let you know as soon as possible."

Give yourself time to grow in your intuition. It might prove to be a unique strength of you.

And an asset for your work.

Intuition as a power of creation

I once read an article in the newspaper about a famous French perfume company. In this company one woman was called the NOSE. She had the unique talent of being able to smell incredibly well. She created the perfumes for the brand. And when I read the way she did it I thought--Wow. That is amazing. They gave her one year to discover and play. With new themes, new ingredients. To create a new perfume for the brand. A possible success. They gave her all the freedom she needed to create.

Starting with just a small idea. Like a seed. To explore it, play with it, finding new combinations. Creating her unique masterpiece.

I know having a year of freedom to create something new is not possible for everyone. But the main ingredient of all this is having the freedom to play. To be open and explore during the process of creation. Finding ingredients you like, trying new things, opening up for new ways and ideas to become real.

In this process of creation there is no failing. There is only exploring.

By creating this freedom, it opens your mind. To find new ways that you would not have seen before.

So, I think it is a good idea to invite intuition at work with open arms.

Questions:

Do you use your intuition at work?

How could you facilitate yourself to express your intuitive ideas?

Have you ever spoken with colleagues about intuition at work?

12
BODY AWARENESS

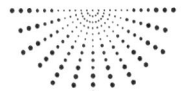

HOW DO YOU RECONNECT WITH YOUR BODY?

Body awareness is a very important capacity that many people seem to have lost.

Daily practice can reestablish this relationship in an easy and pleasant way.

I have collected some good practices that can increase your body awareness.

Enjoy!

Observe

See and treat your body as a dear friend and check in daily. On a regular basis, have a conversation by asking: How are you? What do you need, how do you feel? What can I do for you?

Breathing

How is your breathing? Just observe the way you breathe. Is it high or low in your body?

You can use your breath as a wonderful stress release. Just breathe in life energy and breathe out everything that no longer serves you. Practice this a couple of times.

You can also try some breathing methods like the Box breathing of 4x4. Breathe in for 4 seconds, hold for 4 and release your breath for 4 seconds by blowing out of your mouth as if you are blowing through a straw, finally hold your breath again for 4 seconds. Repeat this sequence a couple of times.

Stress Release

Observe what happens with your body in times of stress. Just be aware of your body signals. Like the way you breathe, the way you sit, stand or move. And the way you feel.

Be aware of your inner dialogue. What do you say to yourself? Are you behaving like an inner drill sergeant? Are you treating your body with respect?

Is there anything you could do for your body to make it feel more comfortable?

For example:

- Change your position.
- Consciously breathe in and out. Especially in times of stress, sometimes we hold our breath and forget to breathe out. Breathe out and release everything that no longer serves you!

- Feeling your feet on the ground.
- Practicing some shoulder rolls.
- Stretch your arms up to the sky and make a circle around you.

Shaking

Did you know that shaking is a wonderful practice to release stress?

Animals who have stress do it and it is an interesting practice to copy.

Like an antelope that has been chased by a lion. After running for her life, she starts to shake all over her body.

As a stress release. We as humans usually don't do this, but we should. Because if we don't release stress from our bodies, it will stay there.

So, let's shake!

You can put some nice music on, or even without is possible. Just stand up and start to shake your right foot- then go up while shaking your right leg.

Shake your left foot and left leg.

And then move up and start shaking your hips, upper body, arms and head. Just release all the stress out of your body. And have fun.

Do it for a couple of minutes and smile.

You can do this as a daily habit and see how it makes you feel.

Joy

Equally, it is important to be aware of your body signals in good times. Your body also provides us with all kinds of signals when you enjoy life.

And your body will tell you when you are on the right track, as your inner guide's compass.

So, where in your body do you feel when something is good for you?

Maybe you can remember a good decision that you have made. Do you remember the body signals you had?

All these daily practices are helpful in raising your body awareness and establishing your relationship with your body as your best friend.

In return your body awareness will guide you to make the best out of your life.

Questions:

How often do you check in with your body?

What daily practices will you add to build a new relationship with your body?

Try the various exercises and journal about how they make you feel.

- Treat your body as your best friend
- Observe your inner dialogue
- Box Breathing (explained above)
- Shake your body practice

13
INTUITIVE CREATION

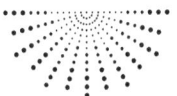

On Mother's Day 2024 our twenty-four-year-old daughter surprised me with a unique gift: A lovely card with an invitation: "Mom let's spend a creative afternoon together and make our own paintings!" She supported that idea with a bag filled with all kinds of creative materials. Two white boards, a box filled with 30 different colors of paint and a variety of brushes.

A month later was our creative day. We both set at one side of my kitchen table, with all our materials in reach. We had some nice music on, light some candles and both had a cup of tea, we were all set.

My daughter asked, "what are you going to create mom? Do you have a plan?"

Suddenly I realized in all my excitement about spending creative time together with my daughter, I had prepared the room, but I had not thought about preparing an idea. I suddenly felt as if I was back at school and had forgotten to do my homework.

My daughter instead had a plan and knew what she wanted to create. She had a photo from a magazine with an image she loved, and even some ideas of the creating process. She asked, "Do you have a hair dryer mom? I want to experiment with splashes of paint and then air dry them. I am so excited to find out what will happen. It might be a fun way of creating!"

She was filled with enthusiasm. And I felt the opposite. For a moment I felt blocked, as if I had done something wrong.

As you can imagine, I did not enjoy that feeling. It was not helping my creating process at all.

So, what to do?

While my daughter was busy with her painting, I just sat at the table and took a moment to be in the NOW. To accept how I felt and what had happened. I was tuning myself in and out, to reflect on the present moment. And I realized what had happened. And smiled about it.

Yes, for a moment I did feel like I had done something wrong. As if I had failed to prepare and did not meet the expectations. As if I had to be and act differently than I was.

But was this the truth?

I realized my daughter had no expectations of how I had to create my piece. It was going to be my creative journey. And the beauty is that we are all different. There is nothing wrong with having different approaches in creating. As an extension of the way we are. In fact, I saw it as an interesting invitation to find out more about my way of creating. So, the first thing I did was accept the situation.

Secondly, I asked myself the question: "What do I need to enlighten my creating process? What would be helpful right now?"

I closed my eyes for a moment. I felt my feet on the floor and felt into my heart. I took some easy breaths in and out.

Spontaneously, an idea popped up. I walked to the closet and intuitively grabbed one of my card decks, a deck with beautiful colors, one that I use for myself and my coaching sessions.

The card I blindly chose was about *BABY STEPS* with the text "follow your intuition before it makes sense."

The text helped me to relax and to be in the playing mode. I looked again at all the beautiful paint colors we had on the table, and realized they looked like a treasure box. I took one color that was appealing to me. Off I went. For 2 hours I created in a flow, listening to my intuition, without a strict plan. I just listened to the ideas that popped up, trusting the process and letting it happen step by step. I can tell you, being in this allowing and playful mood helped me to have a great time. From being stuck, I was now fully enjoying every step in the process.

Occasionally my daughter or me had a short moment where we felt stuck. But we found a great solution. To pause for a moment, relax, reflect and ask ourselves what could be helpful. Then we listened to the spontaneous ideas popping up.

We were inviting our playing energy in.

After two hours we had both created our own unique piece with our creative signature. By allowing ourselves to be present and to find our own ways in the creating process, we both had a wonderful time together. And on top of that we both loved the final results!

We followed our own paths and learned more about our creation process and about each other. Yes, we were definitely different types of creators, and it was all good.

How can you find your authentic way of creation?

Did you know we all have our unique ways of creation? It can be interesting to learn more about finding your own way. What do you need to be in that playful mode? What gives you ideas? What helps you to be in a flow?

You can create your sacred place of creation. You can turn on your favorite music for the background, add a nice smell and maybe some candles.

Another idea to find out your unique way of creating is the try and error method. You can try out different approaches to creation. Like with or without a (strict) plan. Or anything in between to find out was suits you best.

When you cannot find your flow, it can be helpful to acknowledge it without punishing yourself. To be aware of what you tell yourself before, during and after the creating process. A good question is: "Is it helpful what I am telling myself?" If not, then stop and change the comment into the question: "what could be helpful for me right now?"

Especially when you have a desire to create guided from within, it is essential to be in connection with yourself. To be open, to be able to listen to your intuitive insights and ideas without prejudices. To allow and facilitate yourself to be in your creative flow. And to realize it is not important to know the destination of your creative journey. All you need to do is to play and trust.

By exploring all of these, you will find your perfect ingredients of your unique way of creating. Allowing yourself to create out of joy and flow, listening to your intuition. So, you can be the best facilitator for your unique creation process. With better results and so much fun. Because the more you realize this, the more you can allow yourself to explore the unique creations that want to be expressed through you.

I believe we are all creators. Whether you see yourself as a creative person or not. Because you don't have to be a famous painter or fashion designer to be a creator. When you look around you, all the things were once an idea that popped up in somebody's head. And all these things had a creative journey.

I see the art of creation as something magical. How an idea pops out of nothing in our head or body, with the capacity to become real. Like a seed that contains everything inside. And needs some water, love, light and room to grow. However, when you don't pay attention to the idea, it just flows away. And might land through another person.

Therefore, it is important to explore your ideas and to find out your unique ways of creation so you can express your authentic self in your ideas. Your creations are a way to shine your light.

Questions:

When are you creating in a flow?

What do you tell yourself during the creating process?

What can you do to invite playfulness in?

NOW

*"To the mind that is still,
The whole universe surrenders."*
Lao Tzus

14
THE PRESENT IS A PRESENT

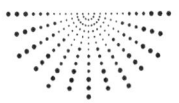

The past is history; the future is a mystery,
and the present is a present.

Maybe you have heard this saying. I think it is an important thing to remember daily. Did you know most of our thoughts are about past and future? Somehow, we find it hard to be in the now.

What if we could truly see the present as a present?

To me it means to be in the moment with every vessel of my body. To truly see, feel and listen with attention. It's my way to live life fully. I do this as much as possible and sometimes the present is just perfect.

Can you remember moments in your life that just felt perfect?

When I think back on my happiest moments in life some

moments flash up. And because I have lived them so fully, I can always recall them.

Let me share some with you.

Family road trip through Australia

To celebrate our ten years of marriage, we took our kids on a journey to Australia, a journey we all will never forget. For us Europeans, the other side of the world.

Since my husband and I had been traveling there before we got married, it was like the circle was round again. To go back there with two kids, nine and six years old at that time, it was a wonderful opportunity to see our family in Sydney again, a family that we had not seen for such a long time.

We had an adventurous holiday for four weeks. The school gave us an extended holiday, if our children would do their homework during the trip. Our traveling was filled with adventurous and wonderful moments. We danced around the Christmas tree with our family, saw highlights in Sydney and Perth, cycled around Rottnest Island and then we continued our road trip by campervan.

The campervan was a great way to travel. The kids had their own space in the top floor and our campervan felt like our own little home whilst traveling.

Our days started with schoolwork, so we would have the rest of the day off for fun things. One day I was helping the kids with their schoolwork in a Natural Park.

We were sitting there at a picnic table, with no people around, surrounded by nature. Our so-called, outdoor classroom of the day. At one point we heard a strange noise, and it was coming closer. We had no idea what it could be.

Within a couple of minutes, we were surrounded by a group of kangaroos. We all had never seen kangaroos in the wild. So, we were all excited. They watched us from a distance and moved on.

We all realized this road trip would teach our children so much more than just being at school.

We drove from Perth, West Australia, all the way up to the North, sometimes driving long distances. I remember the sign on our navigation telling us we had to drive 450 km straight ahead. We had never experienced that before. Our final destination was Monkey Mia, the highlight of our trip. Monkey Mia is located in the Shark Bay World Heritage Area and is famous for its dolphins. Every morning wild bottle-nosed dolphins would come close to the beach in shallow water, where children could feed them fish under ranger supervision. It was the cherry on the cake for our trip. The children were so excited and looking forward to this experience.

When we arrived at Monkey Mia we had found a great camping spot, and we had spent a beautiful day at the beach. It was evening and I had just done the laundry. I walked back with the basket with our clean laundry in my arms towards our camper. I could see my husband sitting in front of our campervan with a cup of tea for both of us. He had just put the children to sleep. They were probably sleeping with a big smile on their faces of excitement for the day to come.

Above us was the night sky filled with stars.

Why do I remember exactly that moment?

That moment I realized: I am perfectly happy now. The past, future and present were all just perfect.

I looked back at the three-week road trip we spent together as family having experiences we would never forget. Traveling together in Australia on the other side of the world, experiencing a different culture, habits and the wideness of the country. The paradise beaches, exotic birds and other animals. Most of all, being here as a family, exploring beautiful Australia was just magical.

The future was perfect. The next morning the children would fulfill their dream. Meeting wild dolphins and even feeding them!

My day had been perfect. We all had a fun day at the beach of Monkey Mia. On top of that, whilst snorkeling I had a spontaneous encounter with a dolphin. A wild dolphin came close to me and looked me right in the eye. It is a moment I will never forget.

Therefore, the past, present and future were all wonderful!

That moment, walking towards my camper, with my fresh laundry in my arms, looking at the bright stars, I realized life was perfect, exactly the way it was. I was breathing in happiness. Joy, love and gratitude was in every cell of my body. The funny thing is, because I was so present at that moment, I can recall it so well that I can still feel it. It is like an imprint that lasts forever.

Yes, the present is a present.

Questions:

Can you recall a moment of complete happiness?

Go back to that moment and journal about it. Where were you? How did you feel? What did you do?

Where do you feel it in your body?

15
WOMEN'S RETREAT IN ITALY

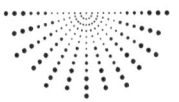

What happens when you put thirty-six women together on a silent retreat on the top of a mountain in Italy?

When I received the invitation to join this women's retreat in Italy, my heart was jumping from joy. Although not much of the program was shared in advance, I trusted my intuition and I knew I had to go. So, I made it possible.

The retreat center was a beautiful resort with a big temple, a garden, an indoor swimming pool and spa. The view was incredible with a lake, the mountains and a picturesque old Italian village.

I was invited, together with thirty-five other women. We were diving in feminine energy for a week. During this week, we were not allowed to drink coffee, alcohol or to eat meat or fish. A cook prepared the most wonderful vegetarian dishes for us. Incredible what he could do with veggies! And besides that, we were in silence for five and a half days. Just imagine thirty-six women being silenced for so long. Would we be able to do that?

Have you ever been to a retreat where you had to be in silence?

This women's retreat was intense with a program from 7am to 9:30 at night.

At seven o'clock we started the day with a glass of warm water with lemon juice and a ginger shot to clean our kidneys. The daily program included meditation, yoga, breathing sessions, ceremonies, teachings, dancing and more.

Being in silence also meant putting away our phones in a locker. My family had an emergency number just in case. So, I would be able to leave everything behind and to be in the moment as much as possible. This week was going to be ME TIME.

Being in silence was not hard at all. I even enjoyed it. The first time I ate without speaking felt a bit awkward. But we got used to it, we just sat alone or together at a table and enjoyed our food or wrote in our notebooks. Being a couple of days in silence was intense and wonderful. It made me more aware of all the things our mind usually does, all day long. It is interesting to experience and to reflect on. What will happen if you skip the usual distractions? From phone, TV, social media and even the talks we have.

Just imagine we have between 60-80 thousand thoughts a day and most of them are about the future or the past. We're all doing that, and it keeps us from being in the now. Not to mention the non-stop voice we have of our inner critic who has an opinion about everything we say, think and do. A teacher at the resort said, "your life is a cumulation of *NOWS*, present moments, and if you pass them well, you will have a wonderful life."

Just imagine, when it's quieter in your head and you find a way to release yourself from the inner chatter.

So many things can stop us from being in the *NOW*. It is too quiet that wave of thoughts, even for a short moment of time. It is an experience of being in the now. When everything is just as it was meant to be.

Being together for a week with this group of women that I did not know before, made me realize the magical things that can happen when we as women come together and create a safe space for female energy. To trust, receive and connect. The effect on me of this women's retreat was massive. It made me feel more open and closer to myself. More connected to my body, mind and soul. It's hard to put words on it but it definitely felt wonderful.

And it made me even more aware of the beauty and need of silence. The importance of inviting silence in our daily lives. Which I do on a daily basis. When I am driving my car, I intentionally don't put any music on or other devices. I also enjoy silence during walks or meditation.

The fact that we were experiencing this all together as a group of women, made it extra special. It created a bond in a profound way. We all felt like our hearts were more open.

How did it change me? That is a good question which I cannot answer directly. But I know it has been a great battery charger on a body, mind and soul level.

So, if you ever have a chance to experience a retreat like that, and your intuition says YES, jump out of your comfort zone and do it.

Questions:

Did you ever say YES to something intuitively?

How was it?

What could you do to invite more silence in your daily life?

16
THE EMPTY SPACE

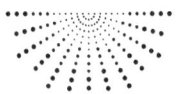

Why are we so afraid of empty space? Time that is not filled with anything at all. It seems like we are not used to it anymore. Time must be productive, filled with things, every minute of the day.

If you meet someone and ask the question "Hey, how are you?" The usual answer is: "Fine. yeah, I am busy." That seems to be the right answer. But is it? At the same time, when we are honest, we often complain about not finding enough rest. By not having time to do the things that recharges our battery. Really fills it.

A friend of mine wanted to step out of the rat race to find out how it would be. She took the adventurous step to walk the Camino, a famous pilgrimage leading to Santiago de Compostela in Spain, Europe.

There are dozens of pilgrimage routes leading to this place all marked with scallop shells. Routes that were often used in the

Middle Ages. She started her walk in Portugal and walked for three weeks, all the way to Santiago de Compostela in Spain. A route of 174 miles/280 km, she traveled light with a small backpack of 7 kilos.

I picked her up from the airport. When I asked her "How was it?" She replied, "Wonderful! and you know what, my greatest gift of walking the Camino was BEING IN THE NOW!

No telephone, no news, just walking together with my friend for three weeks. Often just walking without talking. It felt like it opened up all my senses. I was smelling the roses and admiring the view. Really taking time to stand still, to look, smell and feel. I definitely can say that over these three weeks, we were really enjoying the moment."

It made her and her friend realize how filled their daily life usually is. We all have learned to manage our time and to use it as much as possible in a productive way. To see our daily time in blocks. There is a block for work, buying groceries, household, sports, family/friends and so on. Even a block for holiday time. And some people even plan their holiday time fully. As an example, I have met people who want to see all of Europe in just two weeks' time. It makes me wonder. Can you really be there when you run from place to place? Are you really experiencing where you are, and can you be in the moment? Or is it a recipe to be stressed while you are on holiday?

I believe many people are so busy in their lives that they are forgetting one important thing, to invite some empty space.

What do I mean by empty space?

There can be empty space in your agenda. In your mind and in your body. In fact, for our bodies, it is a natural state. When you look at the way we breathe, there is always a natural state of nothingness. A state in between breathing in and breathing out. This is for a reason. It is a state of allowance and resetting. It's in fact a natural moment of recharging. Our bodies know this. But why don't we do this on more levels in our life? I believe somewhere we have lost this natural way of recharging because of the pressure we put on ourselves. And the fear of empty space, of doing nothing, and just being.

When I look back at my childhood, just being was a normal thing. My agenda was not fully blocked. But I always found something nice to do or just to dream away. And my imagination was taking me everywhere. Yes, at that time we did not have cellphones or the urge to be online 24/7. What a blessing!

There was more connection with us and the environment. When we took a train or bus ride, we were just looking at the view, daydreaming while time was passing by. Do you remember that feeling? Can you recall how normal it was to meet people while traveling. Now everybody is just occupied with their phones.

Do you remember the fun you had as a child lying on your back in nature and just watching the clouds pass by. Using your imagination to discover the most wonderful images in the sky.

Do you still practice this skill of imagining?"

I believe it is important to give more room for this empty space, in your agenda and in your mind.

*It will recharge your energy.

*It will help you to really be in the now.

*It will help you to open up your inner channel for creativity so new refreshing ideas can bubble up!

Therefore, I invite you to create some more empty space in your daily life. Try some silence, just dreaming away time, playing time, or a silent walk.

Find your ways to be more in the now. Just be.

Questions:

How could you allow more empty space in your life?

What can you do to be more in the now?

17
THE ENERGY OF TRUST

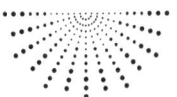

"Mom, I know what I want for my 20th birthday", our son said one day, "let's go skydiving together!"

Wow, this came as an unexpected request. I swallowed for a moment and then heard myself saying, "Yes! Let's do that."

So, to go skydiving was not on my bucket list. But I felt honored to be asked by my son. My husband and daughter went skydiving for her birthday as well and they survived. So, I felt like I could jump into the energy of trust. I would probably survive it.

I certainly was going to need a full bucket of trust. Whilst booking we were upgraded to the highest jump possible, from 13000 ft. The so-called EXTREME tandem Skydive with a free fall of 60 seconds.

Have you ever had an experience where you had to dive deep into trust? A time you felt as if you were jumping into the big unknown?

Fortunately, the sky dive company provided some information about the coming jump adventure, which gave me some reassurance. I would be hooked up to an experienced instructor who would look after me and the parachuting.

The day came for our jump adventure. To my surprise I had a good night's sleep. I really felt like I could do this. Instructions about the jump were provided, and then the group was taken in a small sport plane, up into the sky above the island of Texel in the Netherlands.

I was really enjoying the moment, being there with my son, climbing high in the sky in this little airplane. A new experience that we were both sharing. And my heart was jumping fast for what was about to come. When we reached the exact height of 13000 ft, they opened the door. Immediately a big wind was blowing in the cabin of our small plane. This was for real.

That moment of jumping out of the plane, the moment you let go, that is the hardest part people said. Would I dare to jump?

First my brave son and his instructor jumped. And then it was my turn. No way back. I said a couple of positive affirmations to myself and then we took off into the sky. Our free fall went so fast, just like a rocket.

To be honest, I did not really enjoy the free fall. I felt like my cheeks were somewhere in my ears. The wind was blowing so hard, I could hardly breathe.

But after one minute this changed completely. My instructor opened our parachute, and a peaceful feeling came over me. We slowly went down to the ground. I could finally really take the time to enjoy the scenery of the island and sea beneath me. It was beautiful. With a big smile on my face, we landed safe and sound on farmland. I felt so proud.

My son had already landed.

I could not have had this experience without trust. Trusting that I would be safe. Trusting in my body. Trusting that no matter how the experience would be, I could manage it. And trusting that this would be an experience my son and I would never forget.

And why do I share this?

I notice more and more that trust is an important energy that is declining.

We seem to lose trust and want to have control over as many things as possible.

In some cases, this is needed, for example it is necessary to have control over your car when you are driving. Often however, the need for control is overstated. And it can be demolishing and stop you from living life fully.

The truth is the idea of having control is often an illusion. There are so many things that we cannot control completely. Do you know the saying, *life is happening to you while you are busy making other plans?*

Sometimes pivotal things can happen in your life that just change everything. Have you ever experienced that?

Therefore, trying to control everything is in fact a loss of energy. You try but it is just not possible. So why would you do it? You can use your precious energy better for other things. Like being in the moment and enjoying life. Trusting the process of life. Trusting in yourself and your ability to jump in the deep.

The good thing is that trust is like a muscle. The more you practice it, the stronger it gets. Strong trust muscles can be beneficial in so many areas of your life.

Life is so much more fun when you dare to embrace the unknown and live your life fully.

Questions:

Do you dare to jump in the deep?

Do you want to control everything in your life?

How can you invite more trust in your life?

Affirmations:

- I am safe protected and loved.
- I trust my inner guidance and I am open to receive.
- I live my life fully.

EVOLVE

*"We are all visitors to this planet, this place.
We are all just passing through.
Our purpose here is to observe, to learn, to grow, to love..
Then we return home."*

Aboriginal Proverb

18
SPEAKERS ACADEMY

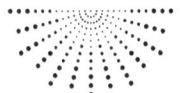

PART ONE - NIGHTMARE ON STAGE

In 2013, I wrote my first book, together with a philosopher, about the art of shining from within. It was a Dutch book, "De Kunst van het Stralen." The media loved it. We were interviewed for many articles in Newspapers, Magazines, had Radio interviews and invitations for speaking opportunities. It was a great time.

Because I knew my speaking abilities could be improved, I joined an academy for public speaking in London. At the Academy we learned all kinds of skills and techniques of public speaking. Like the power of nonverbal communication, the way to stand and move on stage and the art of storytelling.

People from all over the world joined this academy with a variety of professions. For me it was a wonderful way to meet all kinds of interesting people. The training took place in a hotel and each semester was a few days. At one of these semesters, I had joined an intensive five day speaking course. With the last day as closure, a presentation in which each of us could show and prove what we had learned so far.

The last night before the final presentation day, I was preparing my presentation about creativity and flow in my hotel room. In the room next door, I could hear people having a party, drinking, laughing, and talking loudly. It was not the ideal situation to work. But I did my best.

The next day, after just a couple of hours of sleep, it was the day of delivery. The final presentations were held in smaller rooms. We had a group of twenty people. I was 5th in the queue and the people before me did an excellent job.

Then it was my turn. I walked to the front of the room, our stage. Funny how it does not really matter whether the public is massive or not, there is always a kind of excitement walking to the stage. A desire to deliver well, and a bit of stress.

I plugged in my laptop to the system to start my presentation and my worst nightmare scenario came true. The technique totally flipped. Nothing worked. I could feel my heart pounding and my cheeks and neck turn red. I tried all kinds of things without success. A friendly guy stood up from the public to give me a helping hand. Even though he was more technically skilled than me, he could not get the system running.

Did you ever have that experience that everything seems to go wrong?

I wanted to curl up and die.

There I was, standing there in front of this group. They were looking at me with a glance of expectation, wondering what I would do.

So, what do you do when the technique is failing or your initial plan is not working?

How do you stand tall in such an unexpected situation? In the Netherlands we have this expression, *you have to row with the paddles you have*. So that is what I did.

I just took some deep relaxing breaths, in and out. Felt my feet on the ground and looked around me. I changed my state from struggle to acceptance. This became my new starting point. Then I explained the situation to my audience. I used the technique learned at the speaker's academy. To involve your public by asking questions. "Have you ever experienced a situation like this?"

All hands went up.

The Turning point

By acknowledging the situation, what happened and how I felt, I allowed myself to relax a bit and to really be in the moment. And by doing so, magic happened, my creativity started to flow.

I suddenly noticed the extraordinary wallpaper in the room which I didn't notice before. I was happy to see there was a whiteboard in the room and some colored markers. I started using these objects as tools to teach my theory. Right on the spot I created a practical exercise to invite the audience to explore their own creativity. I asked them to solve a question by using the technique of associating. A wonderful way to find new possibilities and solutions. It was very playful, and great ideas came up for them and for me.

The energy in the room changed from stress to joy and playfulness.

In fact, at that exact moment, I was practicing what I preached in a spontaneous way. About the importance of creativity, flow and being in the moment. The power of acceptance. And most importantly, to play and have fun. It turned out to be the most excellent way to teach them about their own creativity and flow.

The audience loved the presentation and gave me positive feedback.

Afterwards I was reflecting on what had happened here. What was my learning point? I became aware of the way I was trying too hard to fit in, to perform in a way that I assumed was expected from me.

And by doing so, I was losing myself and not fully standing in my power.

In one way or the other, the universe took a chance to show me what I was doing by interfering with the technique. It was in fact a wonderful way to make me aware of what I need to stand in my power. It is simply to invite my authentic self forward and to be me.

Questions:

Did you ever experience a situation like that in which you had to deal with the unexpected?

What was it?

What did you discover about yourself?

PART TWO - WOMEN ON STAGE

It was an interesting time, being at this Academy for speakers. I learned a lot about storytelling and speaking skills. It also gave me insights about women and what they need to shine on stage. What is helpful and what can block us. And the importance of safety.

One day we were with three hundred students at the speaker's academy, in a huge venue with a big stage. Talented professionals from all over the world, both men and women.

The teacher did his introduction talk on stage, followed by a special request. He said, "hey guys, before I begin, I would love to hear some of your success stories. If you have one to share, please come on stage!"

Some guys immediately stood up and ran to the stage to talk about their victories and especially how much money they gained. One guy after the other told the same kind of story with even more profit. It looked like a boxing ring, showing their muscles and competing with one another.

I first noticed the effect it had on me. I felt myself shrinking in my chair, feeling small and all kinds of thoughts were crossing my mind. Like, that is not my cup of tea. Is this the right place for my story?

Even if I had a desire to go on the stage to share, it was completely gone by now. I looked around to see what was happening around me.

The energy in the room had totally changed and all the women were shrinking, just like me. In fact, there was not a single woman who went on stage to share her story.

It had become the masculine showing off on stage.

When I realized the effect this was having on the women, I knew something was wrong. I really could not believe that out of hundreds of women, no one had a success story to share. It made me sad and angry at the same time. It was time to take action, so I did.

During the break, I took courage and went to see the teacher. I told him about my observations, and he listened to me with surprise. He had not noticed it himself and he would think about it.

It worked. After the break, I was very glad to hear that the teacher started the program by inviting women, especially, to come on stage to share their story of success.

The first woman came on stage, she had a totally different story from the guys. She started to talk about her desires, her start and struggles on her journey. And she gave practical insights how she had overcome the obstacles that were on the road to her success. She allowed us to be a participant on her journey so we could all learn and grow.

It had a ripple effect, and more women came on stage to share their stories. I felt so much more connected. The energy had changed completely. Instead of competing with one another, we were all participants on our journeys to learn and grow.

So please, when you are in a situation like this, reflect, acknowledge the situation and have the courage to take inspired action.

Acknowledge what you need, and maybe this is exactly what needs to change. You can surely make the difference.

Questions:

What is your definition of success?

Have you ever experienced a situation where you did not feel safe to speak?

What did you do about it?

19
GROWING IN YOUR COMFORT ZONE

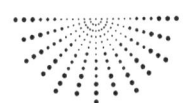

A famous saying states you have to get out of the comfort zone to grow. But is that the truth?

Does growing always have to imply discomfort or even pain?

And, what if that is an illusion?

These were questions I was asking myself when I was recently watching TV.

On the screen was a popular program in which the participants freely agreed to go through extreme physical and mental challenges in a kind of military form. A drill sergeant from the navy coaches the participants to find their own limits. And to go beyond, physically and mentally.

When they fall on the ground, this drill sergeant is yelling, "WHAT ARE YOU DOING? You think you are reaching your limits, but you have more in your tank. Just dig deeper!" And then they usually obey the commands.

We see them falling down in the mud over and over again in heavy rainfall, carrying a huge stone as weight in their backpack, without much sleep. Finding their limits in an extreme way. And after they have passed all kinds of challenges, some of them do reach the finish line. At the end of the program, you see them looking over- exhausted and happy. Proud of themselves, saying they loved every minute of this experience.

These kinds of programs are magnetic for many people, especially young ones, as an example and format for personal growth.

I surely think that this might be interesting for some people. But I do wonder if this is the best strategy for success and personal growth. What are the side effects of this method? What if you only believe in no pain, no gain?

It will definitely have some consequences for your relationship with your body. Because in order to grow in the no pain no gain method, you will have to become a master in pushing your physical signals away, ignoring them fully. So, your inner drill sergeant can take the lead and push you further and further.

I believe that's what happens with so many people in daily life. In order to grow, we push ourselves. We ignore the body signals that tell us to slow down. Maybe when we are extremely fit and physically strong, we can cope with this strategy. But for how long? And what are the side effects?

Your body is no machine.

I believe seeing your body as a machine is unhealthy and will cause some physical problems sooner rather than later.

When you stop listening to your body with respect, you will also lose the ability to receive important information, signals on your life path that lead you, like an inner compass on your way. Information that can help you understand what is good for you and what's not.

When you do listen to your body with respect instead of using a whip, you will receive important signals about what makes you happy, what gives you energy and intuitive insights that can help you in the process of decision making. Like an inner compass.

For example, I usually receive a kind of tinkling feeling in my lip when something is right for me. When this happens, I see it as confirmation of my decision. As support.

Not listening to your body is as if you are ignoring a dear friend who is always there for you. But you don't want to listen to what it has to share.

The possibility is that your body will stop talking to you because you don't want to listen anyway.

Or it will turn up the volume in an extreme way by blocking you physically. Saying STOP, this is enough!!

The consequences are severe pain or even burnout. Is that worth it?

My husband, who is an osteopath, often sees people who have problems listening to their body signals. In his practice he makes them more aware of their bodies and their need to listen to what it has to say. Unfortunately, at school nobody teaches us about the necessity of listening to our body language. So, we have to learn by ourselves, by being curious, willing and open to listen to what it wants to share.

The truth is that many people are focused on their mind and have a desire to control everything. As if their mind is in charge and the body is just a vehicle. By not acknowledging our body as a dear friend who is there 24/7 for us, we lose our body awareness.

This is not only causing a lot of health problems, but also a waste of inner wisdom. Because when we deny the signals our body is giving us, we won't receive the intuitive insights and lose the connection to our inner compass.

Body awareness is a gift to yourself, which can bring you a lot. It opens up the door for your body, mind and soul connection. Therefore, growing IN your comfort zone is a gentle and powerful way to uplift you into your next authentic level of personal growth.

Questions:

Are you a drillmaster for yourself?

Do you see your body as your best friend?

What could you do differently?

20
ANCIENT WISDOM & FEMININE ENERGY

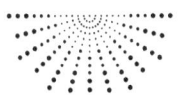

In the summer 2024 my husband and I were delighted to spend our holidays in Greece. Did you know Greece has more than 6000 islands? We were going to do some island hopping, visiting five islands of the Cyclades at the Aegean Sea, with the final destination being the capital Athens on the mainland.

Greece, is a country in Southeast of Europe, known for its clear blue waters, sunny beaches, mountains and white little old towns. And its Culture! The country is filled with treasures from ancient times, with archeological sites and museums. Greece is considered the cradle of Western civilization, being the birthplace of democracy, Western philosophy, the Olympic Games and much more.

Why am I telling you this story?

When we went to Greece, I had no idea that the whole trip would be filled with discoveries, not only of the beauty of the islands, but especially about ancient wisdom and feminine energy. Discoveries of things that I needed to share with you.

It all started at Santorini, the first island of our holidays, on the first day. Santorini is a volcanic island with black, red and white sandy beaches. Little white villages in the mountains with panoramic views. There on the island of Santorini, the theme of the trip was ancient wisdom and feminine energy.

We just had rented a car to explore the island and were driving around without a strict plan. My intuition brought us to a place that we had never heard of before. An archeological site called AKROTIRI. It used to be an important settlement with high culture founded in 5000 BC. In 16th century BC the settlement was buried in volcanic ashes during the Theran eruption. And lucky for us, it is remarkably well preserved. As a visitor it is still possible to walk around in the settlement and to use your imagination about how life must have been when people were living here.

I was impressed. The houses looked modern in a way, three-story buildings with staircases, rooms with a view and amazing frescoes. They even had a drainage system. During the excavation that started in 1967, portable ovens, lots of tools and pottery were found. And the most beautiful jewelry that I still would love to wear today. Walking there invited me to visualize how life was at that time thousands of years ago.

When I saw a building called 'The House of the Ladies' I was really full of awe. One wall was filled with an impressive fresco of three ladies. These women looked like they were important, full of grace, wearing beautiful clothes, long black hair, and golden earrings. The three women were standing with one hand palm up, one arm down. Above their head the sky was filled with stars. I stood there for a moment enjoying the beauty of it all. Realizing, wow, people made this with so much love, centuries before Christ. And then I noticed an important thing, all the stars above these women were connected with each other! When I realized their inter-connectedness I was literally star struck.

Combined with the position of their open palm as if they were receiving wisdom, it made me realize that this might have been the message of the fresco. So above, so below, so within. As a remembrance and honoring of source, connection and feminine energy, was this common knowledge and part of their daily lives? Did they know more about this connection with ancient wisdom than we do today?

There is not much written about females during that time, and what is written is usually written by men. I stood there for a while, letting the power of the image come through me.

I realized the symbolism of it all. As if this inner knowing of connection, their ancient wisdom, was covered with ashes when the volcano erupted. It made me happy and sad at the same time. While I was thankful for being in this beautiful place, and for the insights it gave me, it made me sad to realize that this feeling of connection is exactly what is missing in so many people's lives today. They lost it and don't know how to get it back. Even today, this ancient knowing is what so many people are longing for.

The more islands we visited, the more stepstones were revealed of the ancient wisdom and feminine energy theme. We saw temples and other archaeological sites. Unfortunately, at many places the original feminine temples were destroyed and rebuilt for a castle or church, as frequently has happened all over the world. In this way feminine knowledge and wisdom was replaced by a more masculine dominated society.

The last days of our holiday we spent in Athens, the capital of Greece. I don't know if you have ever been there, but the city heart is filled with treasures from ancient times. Like the Acropolis, high on the hill looking over the city. It contains the remains of several ancient buildings and is on the list of UNESCOs World Heritage.

We booked tickets to the Acropolis at the end of the day, trying to escape the heat. The most impressive to me was the temple of Athena, erected around 420 BC. Athena, the goddess of wisdom and philosophy, peace and the protector of the city of Athens, is often symbolized with an owl and olive tree. The temple was well preserved and had a column with statues of women, all in toga with long hair, proudly standing at the entrance of the temple. I could still see and feel its magnitude. I read that this female temple, although certainly not the biggest one, used to be the most important of the city. Then I saw the olive tree in front of the temple. My husband took a picture of me while I was reaching for an olive, which is a symbol for Athen's wisdom.

On the final day we decided to do something completely different, we dove into some Modern Art. Athens has a huge modern Art Museum, it felt like a jackpot.

When we walked in, to my surprise, I saw the name of the temporary exhibition, "What if women ruled the world?"

Five floors filled with female art! I felt like I was struck by lightning, realizing the coincidence of this.

My husband and I enjoyed it a lot. To see the difference in the perspectives of women about the world problems, about aging, about love and so much more.

It was opening up our minds. One wall was filled with large photo portraits of women over sixty-years-old. Beautiful colored photos, picturing them with so much honor and respect. With the message, why should we look at elder women as if they don't contribute anymore. As if life is over when you are aging?

These women in the portraits showed so much power!

In another floor the documentary "Two minutes to midnight" was showed, really mind blowing. All about the topic "What if women ruled the world?"

The documentary took us to a huge conference room, as we often see when politicians come together to discuss world issues. This time the room was filled with only women, powerful women coming from all around the world. They were discussing world problems. The women were open minded and listening to each other, to the different views and comments. Their views and perspectives were amazing and inspiring. My husband said, "If women could rule the world there definitely would be less war. Women are less ego driven, and not so foolish to react with aggression, like men often do, as if they are always competing with another."

Also, the importance of the way we chose and used our words was mentioned in the documentary. Like the danger of talking about people as if they are TARGETS instead of people. This prevents us from seeing each other as humans, to connect and to open up our minds and hearts.

To me It was a full circle moment. Because I realized I started this journey with the impactful message of connection, when I saw the fresco of the three women in Santorini. So above, so below, so within. To see how many temples were destroyed and replaced with churches and castles. Suppressing female energy and ancient wisdom replacing it for a more masculine dominated society. And the message of the female artists in the Modern Art Museum, to look at the world from another perspective, from love and connection.

It awakened an inner fire in me. It was like the message became clearer to me. It is time for us to wake up and to connect. It is time to invite our forgotten knowledge back, our inner wisdom. To remove the layers and polish the treasures from within. To stop the activation of polarization, as if we always have to compete and struggle. To stop seeing people as numbers and to start seeing each other as humans.

I call it feminine energy and ancient wisdom, which I believe is in all of us, men and women.

It's time to reconnect with this feminine energy and ancient wisdom. To shine our lights and make the world a better place.

Visualization:

Imagine yourself entering the temple of ancient wisdom.

Know that you are so welcome there.

Reconnect with your inner wisdom.

Question:

What does it have to share with you?

21
AND-ALSO

LIFE IS HAPPENING TO YOU WHILE YOU ARE BUSY MAKING OTHER PLANS.

Do you know this phrase? It was so accurate for me while I was writing this book. I just had two dear friends here from overseas, from Australia and the USA. I had planned everything so well for the visit of my friends. I had taken some days off to be able to show them some great places in the Netherlands. When I picked them up from the airport, we felt like three happy puppies wiggling our tails. We had met online during COVID, and this was the first time we finally could see each other's life. It was magical! We went to the market square of Haarlem, enjoyed a tour through the canals of Amsterdam and cycled around the island of Texel on electric bikes.

And on top of that, spending some days with them made me feel like I was a tourist in my own country. I can really advise you to do that now and then. It is refreshing to see things from a new perspective. We had so much fun.

And then life happened. My mother-in-law, who I had been close to for thirty years, was hospitalized and it did not look good. While I had my two friends visiting, at the same time, there was a big shadow of sadness because of the fact I was slowly losing my mother-in-law. Mother of my husband, grandmother of my two kids. A huge family grieves. Everything we had planned became uncertain, out of control.

How do we deal with these things?

During a meditation the words AND- ALSO popped up in my mind. I wrote it down and repeated the words a couple of times, as a mantra. It made me feel more peaceful.

And then some insights came up. It is o.k. to be happy and sad at the same time.

The idea that we often have is that an emotion is overwhelming and controlling us. As if we are either happy or sad. But the truth is these feelings can be shared in one day and even in one moment. And it is all good. We don't have to feel ashamed.

A memory popped up. When I was nine-years-old, my grandfather died. I suddenly remembered at that time, I felt very ashamed to laugh and have moments of joy during his funeral, while we were all grieving. I especially remember one moment. We were driving in a line of black cars behind the car with the coffin, on our way to the funeral place. The car where I was seated was filled with children. Suddenly our driver did a funny thing, he acted as if we were in a racing car. He was behaving in a playful way and I suddenly had to laugh big time, and the tears were rolling down my cheeks. It felt like an enormous relief of the tension. The sadness I felt at that moment turned into huge laughter. I know now what this driver did was a gift. His way of being helpful in the tragedy. I realize now that there was no reason to feel ashamed of my laughter.

With the wisdom and knowledge, I have now, I know all these feelings can happen at the same time. And it is all good.

Even with the tragedy of saying a final goodbye when life on Earth is over, sadness can be filled with enormous love and even joy. Feeling grateful about how that person has touched your heart, your life. What their contribution was to the people around and to the world.

How they shined their light in their own magical way.

After all love is also letting go of somebody and treasuring the beautiful moments in your heart.

For me *and- also* stands for another important thing. The fact that some things in life we cannot control. The idea that we can control our whole lives is one big illusion. However, we all spend a lot of precious time and money trying to control life, because it gives a feeling of security. But the fact is, there is so much that we cannot control. Like nature, other people and these big things in life, when death is coming our way.

You can gain a lot by letting go of this need to control:

- You can experience more joy
- Being in the now
- Spontaneity
- Flexibility

Embracing the *and-also* idea in your life gives you a more stable ground.

Like a tree that bends in the breeze. The more flexible you are, the more open and able you are to adapt to the flow of life. So, you can gain a lot by being willing to loosen up control. To be able to go with the flow, to trust your inner guidance. You do have control over the decisions you make and how you stand in life.

Two days before my mother-in-law passed away, I had a moment of serendipity when I was listening to a podcast, an interview with a famous Dutch artist and song writer telling some beautiful things about the illusion of control. He said, "when I was young, I wanted to control everything, especially every performance. I thought it meant I had to memorize everything, to perform in the best way. To be honest, the performances were more ego driven, I wanted to show off what I knew and what I could do."

The artist letting go of control also influenced his process of creation. "Now I am older and have a totally different approach. Yes, at first, I do prepare and think about what I want to say and share. And then I completely let it go. Because I want to create out of curiosity instead of ego. Before I go up on stage, I prepare in a different way. I feel my feet, I breathe in and out and I get fully in the moment. I feel the energy of the public in the theatre. In this way I allow myself to actually be. To trust that anything that I need to share at that moment, will be shared."

Listening to his story made me realize the importance of letting go of control when you create and perform, *and-also* to trust the process. The results are much more authentic, pure and aligned when you loosen up control and invite creative energy in. And it also means that you are more open to connection with yourself and the audience.

And then the magic of the moment can take place. Then you can really touch people's heart, mind and soul.

Don't' get me wrong, control can be necessary and needed in some areas. But it is certainly good to reflect on how much you let the illusion of control run your life.

Be open to the benefits you will gain when you start trusting and allowing life to enfold.

Questions:

Do you allow yourself the feeling of *AND-ALSO*?

What in life are you trying to control?

What areas of your life can you loosen control?

22
SOUL LIGHT

HOW DO YOU CONNECT WITH YOUR SOUL LIGHT?

Did you know our younger selves held an important key to our souls. But we all seem to have forgotten to treasure that. As children we were spontaneous and pure. But somewhere along the way we have covered that purity with many layers. At school and in society we learn to think and act in a certain way. We learn to be serious and that we have to work hard to be successful. We learn to think rationally, to have a clear vision and goal, and to compete.

In our way of growing up, they make us believe these things are essential to survive in the system of society. So, we adjust and learn to participate in the system. By doing this we tend to lose our connection with our younger selves and the connection with our purest dreams.

Even if we are so lucky to still remember our childhood dreams, we often put them aside and label them as childish and unrealistic.

But is that true?

What if your younger self, your inner child is holding an important key to your soul light?

Would you be interested in becoming reacquainted with your younger self? To reestablish your connection?

What I found out is that our younger self is our closest version to source, to our soul mission and soul light. The light that you are here to bring, your unique contribution to the world. Your inner child holds an important key to that light, to the purest version of you, without all the layers and with knowledge you may have forgotten. So, if you reestablish your relationship with your younger self, she/he can open the treasure box of your dreams.

How wonderful is that!

Let me tell you the story of my soul light.

As a child I had a vision that I had a torch that ignited the inner light of others. Once their light was ignited, they would then pass it on to others. And the receivers would do the same. It would spread light and happiness like the sun. I just assumed that was my truth, I had no idea what it meant and didn't worry about how to translate it into action. I just accepted it, and I truly enjoyed having that vision because it made me feel happy.

This vision to shine in my light and to ignite the inner light of others was a dream that stayed with me when I grew older. Like a small night light.

I had lots of other dreams as well, like becoming a famous professional ballerina, but that dream was not meant to be with my tall physical posture.

Dancing is still something I love seeing and doing though. I am a fan of all kinds of dance performances like flamenco, classical or modern dance. To me dance is a wonderful way to express the soul.

When the years passed by, and I grew older, I did not think much about that childhood vision. Until recently when I was invited on a personal development retreat and all the pieces of the puzzle came together.

The main topic of the retreat was heart connection. There were guided meditations, inquiries, journaling exercises and we danced a lot. The group was small, and the trainers provided a safe environment in which we really could explore. One journal assignment was to first connect with the heart, to really feel it and ask this question: Please tell me what is your ultimate desire?

Being open to my heart and in receiving energy, I just started to write without judgment. I was open to whatever would flow out of my pen. In doing that, my childhood vision was shown. My heart was making a jump from joy. Yes! This is exactly what I want, and the night light became a flame.

Do you remember your childhood dream?

I could really see and feel my inner child, telling me about her vision to spread light with her torch and ignite the lights of other people. They would then use their lights to give light to others and pass it on. I imagined her sitting on my knee, telling me all about it. I could feel her enthusiasm, pureness and love. It was making my heart sing.

I listened to her without judgment. With an open heart. And I told her "Yes, I am here to listen to you. I want to help you. Shall we do this together? Because I definitely need your help!"

Did you know your younger self and you can work together as a team?

I realized that my younger self could help me to connect with my inner light as a clear channel to source. She is the one who can hold my fire of pureness and authenticity. And she also needs me. Me, as a grown woman, I am the one who can translate her vision into reality. To make it practical and real. So, we need each other!

Another insight was that by writing this book, I am fulfilling her dream! It is exactly as she longed for! So, this book is a present for her. And my inner child is delighted about it. Yes, this book is an activation to ignite your inner light.

To tell you the truth, at first, I had no idea what this book would be about. It started with an image of a sun and a soul desire that I could really feel inside. Did you know a soul's desire often waits patiently until you have time to listen to it, to give it some space in your busy life?

I decided to listen, feel and explore what it needed. To provide it in the best way possible. With time, love and without expectations. Like a little seed of a wildflower, that already contains everything inside to flourish. The creation process was an open journey without a straight vision to go from A to B. It was all about listening to my soul's desire and expressing it into words.

How do you manifest your soul's desire?

It is wonderful to be connected with your soul's desire. But what are the next steps to make it real? Let me share my journey of the creation of this book.

How can I be the best facilitator for my soul desire? What does the book need from me to be created?

These were the leading questions in my creating process. I wanted to be the purest channel possible for the newborn book inside. Just like when I was pregnant with my children, I stopped drinking alcohol. And I was open to receive. Wherever I went, I took a notebook with me to write down spontaneous ideas and insight. And by allowing the stories to unfold, the book evolved. The funny thing is, although I am Dutch, the stories popped up in English. All kinds of authentic stories. Did I really have to share them? My heart says, Yes.

When I look back at the journey of my life and the stories that have been shared with you in this book, I realize that every step was needed on my path.

The burnout and change of direction. The growth in body awareness. The trust in my intuition. The reminders of my soul connection and my heart desires, to shine my light guided from within.

I had to overcome the fear of not being good enough. To stop worrying about what other people might think. I had to overcome all kinds of thoughts, obstacles, doubt and being distracted. These are some of the ideas that stop you from taking steps to shine your light.

In my first book, I shared insights and stories from famous Dutch people about the topic of the art of shining from within. In my second book, the multi author book Divine Love, I wrote a chapter in English for the first time. All these steps were essential in allowing this book to come true.

And because of the pure connection I felt with my soul desire, I expanded the muscle of trust. Trusting in whatever comes from my soul mission is a good step that I can lean into, without having to know exactly where it would take me. My heart and intuition will guide the way to shine my soul light. All I need to do be open, listen, trust and act. My mind and creativity can help to make it real.

This book is an important step in shining my soul light and I am open to the next steps that may arise on my journey.

May this book also be an invitation for you to shine your soul light. And to manifest and share the gifts you have inside.

Questions:

Do you have a soul desire?

Do you remember your childhood dream?

Soul light exercise:

Your younger self holds an important key to your soul. So, let's invite her in!

Just imagine your younger self sitting on your lap. Feeling safe and protected.

Invite her for a one-to-one chat where she can share her ultimate heart desires.

And tell her you are there for her. Listen with an open heart and mind. Without prejudices.

Remember, you are the best team.

Journal about your experience.

ACKNOWLEDGMENTS

Dear Reader,

This book is written from my heart to yours. Writing *SHINE* was a beautiful journey of connecting with my soul desire and what wanted to be shared through me. All I needed to do was to be open, curious and listen to a wish from inside that wanted to bloom.

My wish is that this book is an activation and inspiration FOR YOU to reconnect with your inner sun and shine your light. An invitation to be curious, playful and to listen to the guidance of your soul. Who knows what seeds you have inside that are waiting to be born. New ideas and authentic creations that want to be manifested through you.

Are you ready to shine your light?

If your heart makes a jump of an inner *YES*, I would love to support you in reconnecting with your *INNER COMPASS* and the journey of your *SOUL ALIGNED CREATIONS*.

Scan my QR code above.

GRATITUDE

I would like to thank my inner child who helped me in creating this book. My husband Joost, Eline and Thomas who are always in my heart.

Mary Gooden, Yvette Ferris, Taryn van der Merwe, Karen Dark and Yvonne Kroonenberg. All my dear friends, family, clients and all the other beautiful people that have inspired me. And a special thanks for the women of Essentrics.

Thank you all for your love, trust and inspiration.

Cover photos: Ewout Stradmeijer & Laura de Koning

Design: Robyn van der Toorn

ABOUT THE AUTHOR

MARLYS STRADMEIJER

Marlys Stradmeijer is a Writer, Mentor and Inner Compass Coach who helps people connect to their inner guidance and live with clarity, purpose, and joy. Her work is rooted in the belief that when we listen within, we unlock the power to shine from the inside out.

After earning her Master's Degree in Communications from the University of Amsterdam, Marlys began her career in corporate communications. But it wasn't long before she felt called to shift direction—toward deeper, more soul-centered work. Over the years, she has trained in a wide range of modalities, including Body Language, Shiatsu, NLP, and Voice Dialogue, blending these with her intuitive skills to support personal transformation. She is also a certified Akashic Record Master Consultant.

Marlys is the author of *De Kunst van het Stralen (The Art of Shining from Within)*, *Divine Love*, and *SHINE*—books that reflect her commitment to self-discovery, inner truth, and conscious living.

Her motto, *"A wish is a portal to something you can truly realize,"* speaks to her belief in the power of intention and the wisdom of the heart.

Marlys brings warmth, presence and deep listening to her work. Her guidance is open, pure, and grounded in experience.

She lives in the Netherlands - Europe and loves traveling, exploring beauty, and celebrating the magic of life.

*'We're here to shine -
and to share our authentic
gift with the world.'*

Website http://shineyourlightacademy.com

facebook.com/marlys.stradmeijer

instagram.com/marlysstradmeijer

linkedin.com/in/marlysstradmeijer

www.ingramcontent.com/pod-product-compliance
Lightning Source LLC
Chambersburg PA
CBHW050641160426
43194CB00010B/1760